SILK QUILTS

*From the Silk Road to
the Quilter's Studio*

HANNE VIBEKE DE KONING-STAPEL

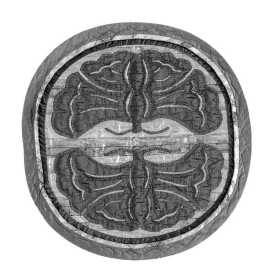

THE QUILT DIGEST PRESS
NTC/Contemporary Publishing Group

Library of Congress Cataloging-in-Publication Data

De Koning-Stapel, Hanne Vibeke.
    Silk Quilts : from the silk road to the quilter's studio / Hanne
Vibeke de Koning-Stapel.
        p.   cm.
    Includes bibliographical references and index.
    ISBN 0-8442-2081-7
      1. Patchwork—Patterns.   2. Silk quilts.   I. Title.
TT835.K66   1999
746.46—dc21   99-18765
                                              CIP

Editorial and production direction by Anne Knudsen
Art direction by Kim Bartko
Project editing by Blythe Smith
Book design by Susan H. Hartman
Cover design by Kim Bartko
Cover photograph by Sharon Hoogstraten
Drawings by Hanne Vibeke de Koning-Stapel, Bertil Merkus, and Kandy Peterson
Photography in Chapter 6 by Sharon Hoogstraten
China and Thailand photographs in Chapter 2 by Clea de Koning
Manufacturing direction by Pat Martin

Published by The Quilt Digest Press
An imprint of NTC/Contemporary Publishing Group, Inc.
4255 West Touhy Avenue, Lincolnwood (Chicago), Illinois 60712-1975 U.S.A.
Copyright © 2000 by Hanne Vibeke de Koning-Stapel.
Printed in Hong Kong.
International Standard Book Number: 0-8442-2081-7
00 01 02 03 04 05 WKT 17 16 15 14 13 12 11 10 9 8 7 6 5 4 3 2 1

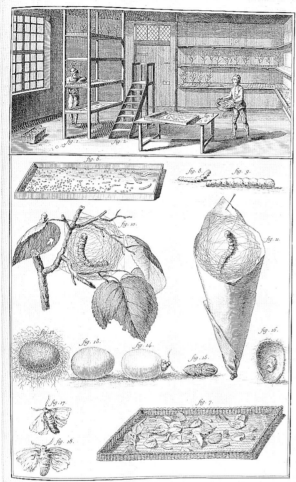

Œconomie Rustique. Vers a Soye

A silk nursery in France, detailing: a
tray with hatching eggs; a basket
with caterpillars eating mulberry
leaves; the silk worm at different
stages of development; a mulberry
branch with caterpillar beginning to
spin its cocoon; a caterpillar
removed to a paper cone cell; a
cocoon with and without floss; a
moth piercing its cocoon; a
chrysalis; the upper- and under-sides
of a **Bombyx mori** moth.
L'Encyclopédie Diderot et D'Alembert, 1762–1772. Planches, dl. I:
Agriculture, Economie rustique, Vers
à Soye. Source: Teylers Museum,
Haarlem, The Netherlands.

DEDICATION

*To the significance of the innumerable insignificant
little silk caterpillars that spin the unexcelled and most
desirable of all fibers into prodigious cocoons, and to all
the diligent hands who unreel and process the cocoons.*

CONTENTS

ACKNOWLEDGMENTS

"When a new grandchild was
announced, I made this white
quilt using a silk/cotton fabric
on both sides. This material
quilts wonderfully and
machine washes well."

Gijs' Quilt
Hanne Vibeke de Koning-Stapel,
1996. 35½" × 43½"
(90cm × 110cm). Hand quilted;
sixty percent silk, forty percent
cotton. Photograph by Sharon
Risedorph.

I am extremely grateful to a great number of wonderful people whose help and contributions were invaluable to the realization of *Silk Quilts*.

It all started with a lecture I conceived on sericulture and quilts made of silk fabrics. My friend of many years, Mary Coyne Penders of Vienna, Virginia, told me that the contents of my lecture made up half a book; why didn't I go on and make a complete book? Mary has accompanied me throughout the whole process; her loving support and interest, her constructive ideas and encouragement, and her never-ending and unconditional assistance have been of invaluable help, for which I am deeply indebted.

My sincere thanks to the quiltmakers and museum curators all over the world who so graciously cooperated by sending slides and giving permission to publish pieces of their work. Special thanks to Mr. and Mrs. van Lerberghe of Belgium and to Atsuko Ohta of Japan, whose help was indispensable in contacting Japanese quilters. Special thanks also to my friends Anne de Vries Robbé, Josje van Duyneveldt, and Nicky van den Berg in Holland, who switched to working entirely in silks in favor of my research.

Special appreciation is due to Boet Christiaanse of Stork Silkscreens who provided my daughter, Clea, and me with contacts in China and Thailand, enabling us to visit silk farms and factories. Thanks are also due to Edward Ong of Hong Kong, who for days accompanied us on our trip to

Wuxi and Shanghai in China. He planned our visits to several silk plants and was our indefatigable interpreter and silk specialist during meetings with Chinese officials. I also want to thank those hospitable officials, whose names are impossible to mention here. However, their willingness to share their knowledge and to allow me to take photographs were a great asset to this book.

In Thailand, Mr. Surindr Supasavasdebhandu of Jim Thompson Thai Silk Company Ltd. and Mrs. Preeda Thamkasem of Thai Silk Development very kindly gave their time and expertise. In Corat the manager accompanied us on the grand tour of the Jim Thompson Silk Plant.

Thanks to Mr. R. Currie of the Association Internationale de la Soie in Lyon, France, and to Mr. A. Faes of the Commission Européenne Promotion Soie in Zurich, Switzerland.

Leen de Jong and Bart Storm of Holland helped me with research on sericulture in Greece and with texts in Greek languages.

In experimenting with the characteristics of silk and with dyeing of silks, these people were always sharing: Meiny Wardenier, Harm Harms, Ineke van Buuren, Agnes Dubelaar, and Ria van Els.

H. J. J. Horsten of Geldrop Textile Museum untangled for me the names of many different silk weaves.

My school friend, Birgit Glüsing in Copenhagen, helped me with the research in Denmark. An Hollis introduced me to quilters in South Africa. Anja Severs and Robert Pruyt were my trustworthy computer companions, always nearby in situations of crisis. Bertil Merkus spent hours with me in front of the computer, drawing the patterns.

During my visits to museums and libraries I was generously helped by textile curators, librarians, and other staff. I want to mention Margriet Winkelmolen of Tilburg Textile Museum, Maria Leimar and Lena Hassel in Kalmar, Virginia Eisemon and Doris Bowman in Washington, D.C., Jacqueline Baudoin-Ross in Montreal, Catherine Noppe in Mariemont, Teresa Tacheco in Lisbon, and Krishna Riboud and her staff in Paris. Elisabeth van Boetzelaer and Judith Helm, also in Paris, Marie-Christine Flocard, Les Loges en Josas, and Janine Benasson-Janniere in Montgiscard were my auxiliaries when my French failed. An Moonen in Westervoort, an expert on antique textiles, was an inexhaustible source of information, sharing generously.

Finally, I wish to thank my family. My husband, our four grown children, and their partners have always been of invaluable support in my periods of cocooning and silky enterprises.

INTRODUCTION

The long history of silk is shrouded in the mystery of the Silk Road that connected the Chinese empire in the Far East with the Greek and Roman empires on the European continent. Stories of adventure, including those of the legendary journeys of Marco Polo and tales of maritime heroes who discovered the sea routes between the Far East and Europe, contributed to a fascination with silk and the sericulture process that has endured through centuries and spread throughout the world. It is my hope that *Silk Quilts* will be regarded as one more step in the fascinating journey—a path that leads to the joy of creating with silk in the quiltmaker's studio.

A QUILTER'S JOURNEY ALONG THE SILK ROAD

When I started making patchwork quilts at the end of the 1970s, I looked for fabrics in Holland. I wanted calicoes and one hundred percent natural fibers. But I was disappointed to find that there were few cottons or even cotton blends of the weight I wanted for my quilts. What I found instead were heavy poplins, decorative chintzes, and many polyesters. Then, one day I came across some lovely, yet affordable, green and white Indian doupion silk fabrics. I bought a few lengths of each color and chose a simple traditional pattern, *Drunkard's Path*, for my first silk quilt; my personal journey along the Silk Road began.

I came to silks with very few preconceptions. It did not occur to me to think of them as too fragile, too delicate, or too expensive for quiltmaking. I had no desire to sew the kind of quilts that are made for warmth as bedcovers, or for the wear and tear of daily life. Nor did I think of making family heirloom or heritage quilts that need to survive for posterity. Fears of silk's fragility—that it is difficult to piece and that it rapidly deteriorates—have made quiltmakers hesitant to use silk, but the more I found out about this remarkable fabric, the more convinced I became that these and other fears are ungrounded. I discovered early on that some of the oldest surviving quilts in the world are made of silk, proof that it is a fabric that keeps its strength and ages beautifully. I quickly learned that silk is a wonderful medium for quiltmaking; it handles well and it endures through time. I knew that other quilters, too, would fall in love with silk, just as I had, if only they knew more about this seemingly mysterious material. This was how *Silk Quilts* began.

A Tribute to the Tiny Silkworm

Silk is not only amazing in its technical properties, but also in its unique origins. For the wonder of silk, we are indebted to an unassuming little creature who works as a living chemical factory. In less than forty days, the humble silkworm produces the filament that becomes silk. Modern technology has for decades tried to discover the secret formula of the silk caterpillar's astonishing production, without success. There is no substitute for real silk, sometimes accorded the lovely appellation of "woven wind," and no chemical factory can reproduce what the silkworm does so well. *Silk Quilts* is my tribute to this tiny, remarkable creature.

CHAPTER 1

THE STORY OF SILK

"A Japanese hostess gave me a piece of very orange gold brocade. I appliquéd an imperial khamon (a family crest) of two bees onto it. I was inspired by the exquisite work of Japanese quiltmakers and by the kimono silks I had bought during an early morning visit to a flea market in Kyoto."

Khamon
Hanne Vibeke de Koning-Stapel, 1997. 55" × 54½" (140cm × 138cm). Hand and machine pieced, hand quilted; Japanese kimono silks, brocade, silk scraps. Photograph by Sharon Risedorph.

The Yellow Emperor was ruler of one of the first Chinese dynasties, around the year 2640 B.C. As legend has it, one day his young and beautiful empress, Xi Ling Shi, was sitting quietly, sipping tea beneath a mulberry tree. A cocoon fell from the tree into her cup and the empress watched as it started to unravel in the hot liquid. Cautiously, she pulled out the thinnest, most gossamer thread any imperial person could imagine.

SILK IN THE FAR EAST

As enchanting as this tale is, archaeologists and historians agree that the cultivation of silk moths did not start with the empress's tea cup. It is certain, however, that the domestication and cultivation of the silk moth began in China more than five thousand years ago. For many centuries, the empress was the patroness of silkworms, and both she and her ladies-in-waiting were active in the cultivation of the *Bombyx mori*, the Latin name for this cultivated moth. It was domesticated for sericulture, the cultivation of silk cocoons. At an early stage, it became evident that the best quality silk came from caterpillars that were fed the leaves of white mulberry trees, called *Morus alba*.

The Chinese kept their knowledge of sericulture to themselves for more than twenty centuries. A death sentence was mandatory punishment for divulging the secrets of the domesticated silk moth. Only the Imperial Court and the privileged nobility were allowed to wear silk. From the beginning, silk was extremely expensive and exclusive.

Early Trade Routes

During a period of political instability, when China was continuously attacked from the north and west by nomadic tribes from Central Asia, the building of the Great Wall was begun. In 138 B.C., Emperor Wu-ti sent Chang Ch'ien, a young confidant from his court, with a small force of his strongest warriors on a reconnoitering mission to Central Asia. Although the military objective of this mission was a failure, and Chang Ch'ien did not return to China until thirteen years later with just one remaining warrior, his journey was historically important because it signaled the opening and subsequent development of trade routes between the two superpowers of that time: the Empire of China in the Far East and the Greek and Roman empires in the West.

Chang Ch'ien had traveled as far west as Mesopotamia and Persia. He gathered valuable information on geography and on the economies of the kingdoms and tribes of Central Asia, explored the rich cities of Samarkand, Bukhara, and Merv, and discovered the amazing horses of the Ferghana Valley. These horses were of "heavenly" stock, they were quick, strong, and manageable, and they sweated blood. Emperor Wu-ti was eager to acquire some of these horses and he was ready to exchange one of his most precious products, silk, to possess them. One of the first regular trade transactions between East and West took place via a network of roads

Ancient Silk

The story of silk is so old that it reaches further back in time than recorded history. Archaeological excavations during recent decades have revealed some of the unwritten history and secrets of silk. In a silk-farming region south of Shanghai, a bamboo basket was discovered that contained pieces of woven *Bombyx mori* silk. One fragment is a quilted piece of taffeta, and carbon dating demonstrates that this find is from about 2800 B.C. Also in China, ritual bronze vessels from about 1500 B.C. have been found with imprints or pseudomorphic images of silkworms. At the same site, archaeologists found twenty fragments of silk in five different weaves: plain and patterned tabby, twill, crepe, and gauze.

In several archaeological sites from around 1100 B.C., polychrome silk compound weaves were discovered with the Chinese character for *jin*, the word for brocade, woven into them, demonstrating that during the Bronze Age the Chinese had mastered the intricate processes of weaving brocade and damask. Excavations of Scythian tombs in Kazakhstan disclosed an embroidered silk saddlecloth, proving that silk was exported from China westward in the fourth to third centuries B.C. There is much more archaeological evidence that silk served mankind in various ways, beginning long before written history, but these examples achieved my goal of finding proof that silk is as old as Methuselah!

that later became known as the Silk Road. The Chinese soon discovered that the Ferghana Valley horses were indeed marvelous, although they sweated blood only because they were plagued by blood-sucking flies. They are immortalized in exquisite bronze and glazed earthenware sculptures.

The End of the Monopoly

The Chinese monopoly on sericulture that had lasted for more than two millennia slowly disintegrated. Around 200 B.C., Chinese emigrants brought sericulture to Korea, and it was through friendly diplomatic relations between China and Japan that *Bombyx mori* silk and the cultivation of domesticated silk caterpillars were introduced to Japan.

The secret of the *Bombyx mori* also moved southwest to India. Wild silk moths were indigenous to both India and Japan, but sericulture of cultivated species was entirely a Chinese enterprise, brought abroad by the Chinese themselves. One legend relates that when a Chinese princess married an Indian nobleman, she was warned that there was no sericulture in her future domicile. Addicted to wearing silks, she smuggled silkworm eggs and mulberry seeds at considerable risk in her silk hairdress. She was thus able to continue sericulture and silk weaving in her new home.

Alexander the Great's Blazing Trail

Asia Minor was, like China, a cradle of highly developed civilization, where the luxury of wearing silk was an important part of the rise and fall of empires and kingdoms. Woven together with the rich history of the Persians, Syrians, and Egyptians are many stories in which silk plays a major role.

Alexander the Great expanded his realm eastward, conquering Tyre, a city on the Asian coast of the Mediterranean, where dyers mastered the exclusive art of producing famous royal purple dyes. Thereafter, Alexander wore only purple silk tunics, much to the distress of his soldiers, who associated purple with their enemies, the Persians.

Another legend tells of the women of the Greek island of Cos. They unraveled pieces of expensive imported silk in order to use the threads to weave a textile that was so transparent it betrayed more of the body than it covered.

A third tale relates the story of the battle of Carrhae in 53 B.C. between the Parthians of Persia and Roman warriors. The Romans lost the battle because they were stupefied when the Parthians surprised them by unfurling lots of colorful, shimmering silk banners.

THE SILK ROAD

Chang Ch'ien's mission started the exploration of ways to reach the Western world from the Far East. Merchants transported their goods on camels from Xi'an, the ancient capital of China, through the inhospitable Gobi Desert. Then they had to choose between the northern and the

The Silk Road
Source: Michael Grimsdale/
Aramco World, July/August
1988, pp. 3–5.

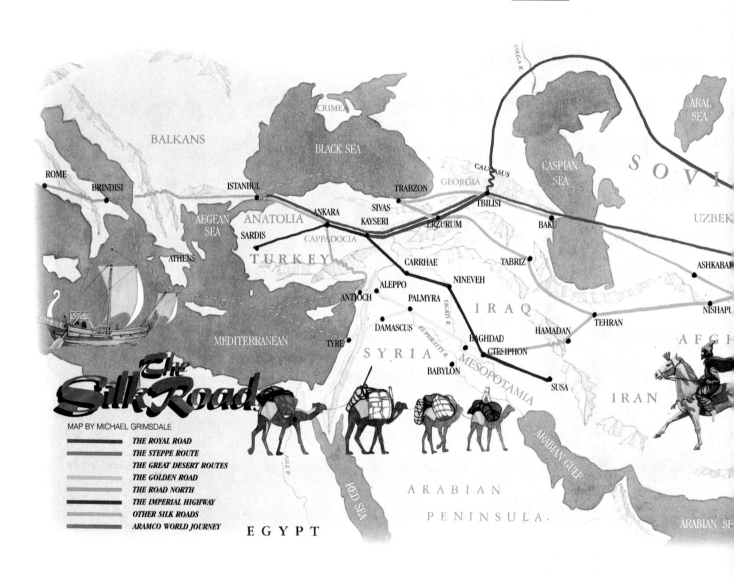

southern tracks around the deadly treacherous Taklamakan Desert to Kashgar, where the two routes met. From this point, the silk route continued through the Pamir mountains, with steep and dangerous ascents and descents to the trade centers of Samarkand and Bukhara, through Persia and Mesopotamia to the Mediterranean east coasts. From here the goods were shipped to Greece, Rome, and Alexandria. This great network of trade routes—which in the nineteenth century was given the romantic name the Silk Road (or Silk Route) by the German geographer and explorer Ferdinand von Richthofen—was put on the map of the world.

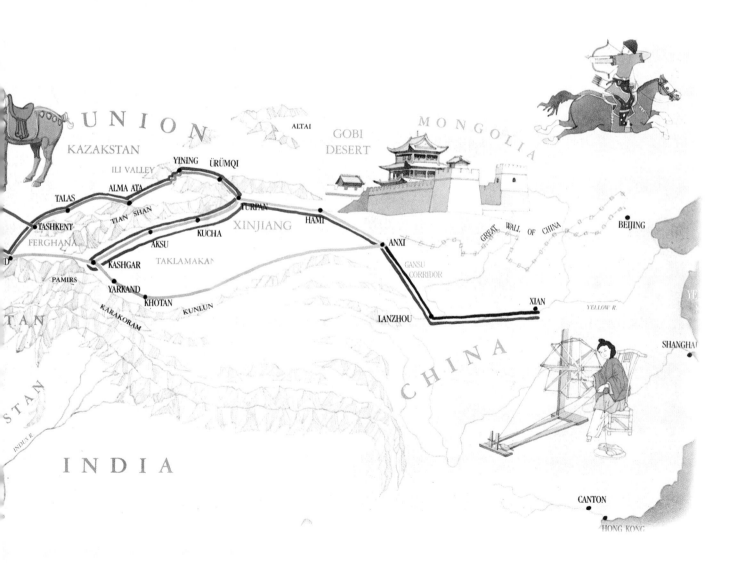

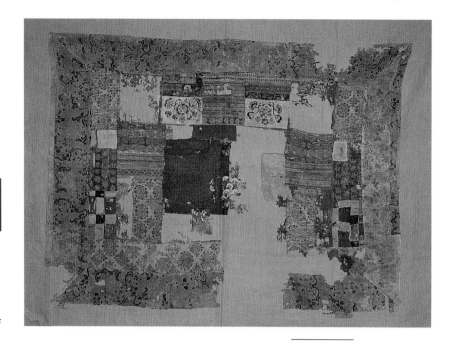

The Rise of Buddhism in the Wake of Silk Trading

Buddhism spread by way of the Silk Road to China from India, where the religion originated in the sixth century B.C. An important collection of antiquities from the eighth and ninth centuries A.D. was discovered in the Caves of the Thousand Buddhas at Dunhuang in China, containing Buddhist silk paintings, manuscripts, textiles, and relics. These sanded-in caves are situated along the Silk Road and were first explored at the beginning of the twentieth century by the Hungarian-British archaeologist Sir Marc Aurel Stein, followed by Swedish, French, and German archaeologists. Almost all the textiles found there are silk. Among the excavated objects was an altar valance of plain, printed, and embroidered silks. Although these altar valances were common in most Buddhist temples, this is one of the few remaining examples.

Also found in one of the Dunhuang caves was a piece of "votive patchwork," as Sir Stein called it. Probably this was a *kesa*, the robe of a high-ranking Buddhist monk.

Buddhist kesa
Source: The British Museum.
Photograph copyright © The British Museum.

Buddhist altar valance
Source: The British Museum.
Photograph copyright © The British Museum.

The Beginnings of Trade

It took a camel caravan many years to travel from China to Europe and back, a hazardous and grueling trip of more than six thousand miles (ten thousand kilometers). Mostly the goods were brought from one oasis or trading post to the next, where middlemen took over with fresh packs of camels. In the Middle East, enterprising intermediaries and agents, especially the Persians, monopolized the silk trade between East and West. No wonder that, once the silk arrived in the Roman Empire, it was as expensive as gold!

Of course, commodities other than silk were traded in both directions via the Silk Road. Porcelain and lacquer, iron and weapons, spices and rhubarb were Chinese goods finding new markets in the West. Return traffic brought glass and amber, grape vines and wool to the East. From Central Asia, horses and indigo dyes were carried in both directions.

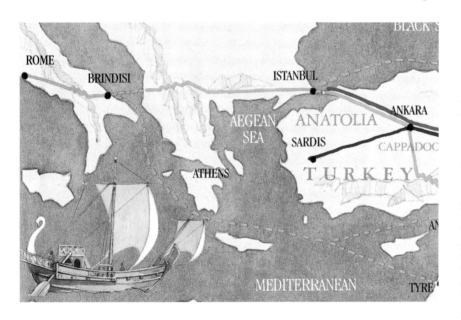

SILK IN EUROPE

After the first silks arrived in the Western world, royalty and nobility in Roman Asia and Europe came to appreciate the luxury of wearing silk. Because the import of raw silk and finished goods was unstable and extremely expensive, a desire grew to produce silk locally. Emperor Justinian the Great of Byzantium initiated the long history of sericulture in Europe in A.D. 552 by sending two Nestorian monks on a secret mission to the East. They brought silkworm eggs and white mulberry seeds back to Byzantium. During their journey they hid the eggs and seeds in their hollow walking sticks.

This was the beginning of sericulture in Europe. Over the next thousand years, these smuggled eggs and seeds migrated all over the Mediterranean area, from Greece and Turkey to Sicily and Northern Africa. The Arabs brought the art of cocoon rearing, reeling, and silk weaving to Spain where, in the tenth century, Andalusia became Europe's main silk-producing center. In the twelfth century, Italy's silk industry began in the northern city states of Lucca, Genoa, Florence, and Venice.

While it was the Arabs who brought sericulture to Sicily and Spain, it was Jewish weavers and dyers from Amalfi in southern Italy who brought their craft to the northern part of the Italian peninsula.

France and England at Odds over the Regal Fabric

Around 1450, Lyon, France, became a major silk-import center. Because this import business drained the country of capital, several consecutive French kings promoted sericulture and patronized the art and craft of weaving silk fabrics with charters and measures of protectionism. When King Henry IV of Bourbon boasted of silk stockings made of French silk, King James I of England became jealous and started a campaign to introduce sericulture in England, in order to be able to boast of English silks.

Sericulture in Europe

Dᵉ CONSTANTIÆ ALAMANNIÆ Nobiliſſᵉ Florentinæ, ex viro ſuo Illᵐᵉ RAPHAELE MEDICEO Florentino,
Hetruriæ pedeſtris militiæ Rectore, liberorum XVI. ſimul viuorun pudiciſsimæ matri,
IOANNES STRADANVS inuentor D.D.

The rich illustrations of Johan Stradanus, a Flemish artist born in 1523, give us an impression of the sericulture process in Europe during the sixteenth century. His designs were rendered into a series of six copper engravings by Karel de Mallery (1571–1635), who worked in Antwerp. The engravings were a gift from the nobleman Raphael de' Medici of Florence to his wife, Constantia Alamannia.

The engraving on this page depicts (counterclockwise from upper left) a silk caterpiller eating mulberry leaves, a cocoon, a moth leaving the cocoon, and a fully developed moth. On the facing page (from top to bottom) the first engraving depicts an encounter between Emperor Justinian I of Byzantium and the two monks who brought silkworm eggs and mulberry seeds from the East. In the second, women nurse the eggs of the silk moths in their bosoms. The eggs are cleaned with wine. In the third, the caterpillers are fed mulberry leaves. In the fourth, the fully grown caterpiller is brought to the branches where it begins cocooning. In the last engraving, women reel the silk filaments off the cocoons.

2. Monachi duo Iuſtiniano Principi   Semen dedere, vermis vnde ſericus.

3. Aſperſa vino terſaq; oua vermium   Papillulis ſolent fouere virgines.

Karel de Mallery,
engravings of sericulture
in Europe
Source: Collection of the
Dutch Textile Museum,
Tilburg, The Netherlands.

4. Excluſus ouo rite vermis, ocyus   Texit ſuam moro inſidens telam arbori.

5. Tum fronde, ramo, faſcibuſq; conditus,   Se voluit, et pila in modum ſe contrahit.

6. Hinc vermium permulta ſæpe millia   Simul legunt, parantq; telas feminæ.

At the beginning of the seventeenth century, James I had tens of thousands of mulberry plants distributed in the British Isles to start sericulture. However, he chose the *Morus nigra*, the black mulberry which grows best in countries with a moderate climate. As we now know, the silk caterpillars prefer white mulberry leaves; the king's ambition to wear home-produced silk stockings was not fulfilled. However, gardeners all over England are still proud to have a descendant of a King James I mulberry tree.

Silk and the Huguenots

Twice within a century, the French silk industry received painful blows. The first time was during the Reformation in the sixteenth century when the Reformed Protestants, the Huguenots, were persecuted. Many Huguenots were expert silk throwsters (workers who *throw*—or twist and double—silk filaments into thread or yarn), weavers, and dyers. But they were not allowed to pursue their trades unless they renounced their Protestant faith. Many were killed; others fled France to neighboring countries, especially England, where Protestant Queen Elizabeth I welcomed the refugees and encouraged them to establish their silk businesses in her country. However, when the French king in 1598 made concessions to the Protestants through the Edict of Nantes, many Huguenots returned to France.

When Louis XIV of France revoked the Edict of Nantes in 1685, the French Huguenots were once again persecuted and fled their country in large numbers. They sought refuge in the neighboring countries of Germany, Switzerland, The Netherlands, and the British Isles.

The contribution of the Huguenots to the development of the silk industries in their new homes was extremely valuable. In England, some Huguenot families settled in Spitalsfield, on the outskirts of London. In a complex that used to belong to the priory of St. Mary of Spital, one of the first English silk mills was established and here the Huguenots continued their skills of silk throwing and weaving.

Silk Becomes a European Industry

In the seventeenth and eighteenth centuries, attempts at establishing silk industries were undertaken in almost all European countries. In The Netherlands, there were already many accomplished weavers and dyers who specialized in processing flax and weaving velvets. In Amsterdam, silk

Detail from **Portuguese Silk Quilt,** *page 49*

manufacturers established themselves and the industry was capable of competing with the French and English manufacturers. City authorities stimulated silk production in order to provide relief work for the poor.

In Sweden, raw silk was imported and several manufacturers produced important quantities of dress and furniture silks, encouraged by the royal court. In Denmark, raw silk was imported and processed into beautiful rich damasks and brocades, encouraged by kings and supported by the expertise of weavers who came from The Netherlands. For a long time, the Russian czars held the monopoly on trading Persian and Chinese raw silk with Europe. In Moscow, there were twenty-one silk manufacturers, and even St. Petersburg had two at one point during the eighteenth century. None of these enterprises have survived, but in numerous palaces and castles, the glorious history of their rich silk heritage is exhibited every day to visitors.

SILK IN THE NEW WORLD

As the silk industry in England developed, it became imperative to import increasing volumes of raw silk. King James I, who had not given up on his passion for silk, decided that his raw silk should come from the Colonies.

Silk in the British Colonies

The soil of Virginia was ideal for growing mulberry trees and the climate perfect for cultivating silkworms. James I shipped silkworm eggs and seeds of white mulberry trees to Virginia and encouraged the farmers to dedicate themselves "to the profitable industry of silk." The king sent English and French sericulturists to Virginia to teach specific techniques of cultivating mulberry trees and of breeding and rearing silk caterpillars. The king's instruction was "to apply yourselves diligently and promptly to the breeding of silkworms, bestowing your labor rather in producing this rich commodity than to the growth of that pernicious and offensive weed, tobacco."

The British intended to have the colonists raise the silkworms and harvest the cocoons, then export them to England for reeling, throwing, and weaving. The English took a liking to the raw silk that the Virginians delivered; in fact, when compared to Italian raw silk, it came out favorably, and many royal dresses were fashioned from Virginia silk. Despite premiums and bounties promised by the Colonial Assembly for engaging in silk production, the Virginia farmers never took a liking to sericulture. They preferred to grow tobacco, which was more profitable.

With the Revolutionary War (1775–1783) came a natural end to silk growing in Virginia. Even so, Martha Washington's dress at the inauguration of her husband as the first president of the United States was made out of silk from cocoons that were grown, harvested, and woven in Virginia.

As silk production waned in Virginia, colonists in the Carolinas and Georgia took up sericulture; it is recorded that they were successful, exporting hundreds of pounds of raw silk each year to England, where it fetched higher prices than Italian raw silk.

Mrs. Pinckney's Cottage Industry

Eliza Lucas Pinckney, who was born in the British colony of Antigua in the West Indies and came to live in South Carolina in 1722, became famous for two achievements. First, she grew her own indigo from seeds that came from Antigua and she knew the complex process of extracting indigo dye. Second, she cultivated her own silk caterpillars; from the cocoons she reeled enough filament thread to have lengths of heavy damask woven and dyed in England—enough for three silk dresses, one of which was presented to the Dowager Princess of Wales.

Mrs. Pinckney's accomplishments in South Carolina were replicated in countless households. In Pennsylvania, sericulture was strongly promoted by the Penn family and by Benjamin Franklin. Well-to-do people, both women and men, dressed up in domestically cultivated rich silks, velvets, and brocades. During the Revolutionary War, ladies were proud to continue cultivating silk cocoons from which they reeled and spun silk sewing thread.

Of all the silk-producing colonies, Connecticut seems to have been the most successful, judged by the volume of cultivated cocoons. A filature was built, where the filament was reeled off the cocoons; in 1771, more than twenty-three hundred pounds of cocoons were processed. The first silk mills for fabric and sewing thread were built in Connecticut.

Detail from Eliza Lucas Pinckney's silk dress
Source: National Museum of American History, Smithsonian Institution, Washington, D.C., U.S.A.

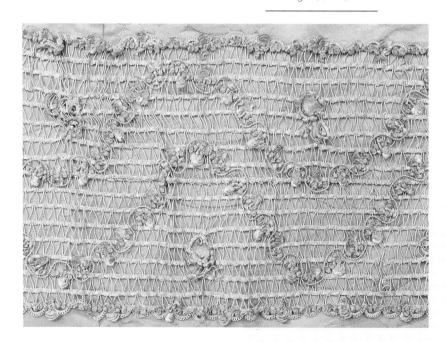

The Tide Turns

After the Revolutionary War, silk manufacturing became a promising industry in America with a steady demand for homegrown cocoons. But it almost fell prey to bankruptcy in the second half of the 1830s because of capital speculation and prospects of quick profits. A new variety of the mulberry family, the *Morus multicaulis*, was introduced and skillfully marketed as a marvel that grew leaves bigger and richer in nourishment in shorter time than the *Morus alba*. Where a *Morus alba* could feed only one crop of cocoons for one season (monovoltine), a *Morus multicaulis* could feed two crops of cocoons (polyvoltine). A wild buying and selling rush began, and when the demand for these new trees exceeded the supply, prices rose steeply. A frenzied rush on tree cuttings ensued, and this caused further upward spiraling of prices, not unlike the famous South Seas Bubble.

When the bubble burst in 1840, causing many hundreds of cases of financial ruin among farmers, dissatisfaction with everything connected to sericulture ran deep. It was easy to conclude that the requirements of extreme patience and long laborious hours producing raw silk, combined with the low and uncertain output, did not suit the American temperament.

Silk in the Spanish Colonies

A century prior to James I's attempts to establish silk industries on the east coast of America, sericulture was introduced in New Spain (Mexico) by the Spanish conquistadores. At the beginning of the sixteenth century, the colonists and missionaries from Andalusia introduced sericulture in many places, profiting from the wild mulberry trees that are indigenous to Mexico. However, sericulture did not develop in Mexico according to Spanish expectations and quickly vanished. Some Spanish missionaries went north along the coast of California, where they established mission posts among the Indians and planted gardens with exotic fruits and white mulberry trees from Andalusian seed. This happened long before the settlers arrived from the east. Sericulture existed in California in the beginning of the twentieth century; before World War II, cocoons were sent to Japan to be reeled. When reeled silk came back, it was made into silk stockings and parachutes.

Mormons, Shakers, and Quakers

A notable exception was widespread silkworm rearing in several religious settlements in colonial America. Raising silkworms was part of community life in these communities, considered a way to provide extra income for a mother with children. The Mormons of Utah profited from the sericulture expertise brought by converts from Europe and Japan; from 1899 to 1900, the Mormons produced seventy-five hundred pounds of cocoons.

From early on, Shakers and Quakers produced silk, some for their own use in scarves and kerchiefs, but also for lengths of fabric for export to England. Queen Charlotte of England wore a dress made of silk produced

Silk Quaker quilt
Elizabeth Smedley, Philadelphia, c. 1891. 84″ × 91¼″ (213cm × 232cm). Brown satin and tan checked silk; pieced. Source: National Museum of American History, The Smithsonian Institution, Washington D.C., U.S.A., 95.7166 T. 1984.1059.

Shaker silks—the second two pieces from the bottom and the piece on the top are silks; the rest are linen.
Source: Shaker Museum and Library, Old Chatham, New York, U.S.A. Photograph by Michael Fredericks.

The Harmony Society

Raising raw silk is part of America's colonial history; I think it is plausible that the silk quilts created during this period were made from the filament of American cultivated silkworms. The most interesting information in this context is about the Harmonists in Economy, Pennsylvania.

Gertrude Rapp was born in 1808, the granddaughter of German Father George Rapp, who came from Württemberg, Germany, with a large group of pious followers. Father Rapp settled in Pennsylvania and started the Harmony School. The Harmonists practiced shared property and believed that through harmony, beauty, and industry they could create Utopia near to God. The Harmonists enjoyed an excellent reputation for manufacturing wool and cotton cloth, and Gertrude wanted to expand this business with silk manufacturing. Gertrude spoke German, but she had learned English while living with the Shakers in West Union, Kentucky, and she also studied French. It was a great advantage that she could read French, English, and German literature on sericulture and correspond with experienced sericulturists in Europe.

Gertrude started at the beginning and supervised the planting of mulberry trees on eighteen acres of land. Silkworm eggs were imported and, by the end of the 1830s, the production of silk cocoons was more than twenty thousand pounds. During the season, children helped to feed the voracious caterpillars, and young girls were taught to reel and throw the raw silk that was dyed with natural dyes and woven into exquisite dress and vesting fabrics. At the silk exhibit in New York, Gertrude Rapp received for the Harmony Society the gold medal for the best specimen of silk velvet and fancy ribbon. However, as the Harmonists lived in celibacy, by 1852 the work force had aged and the silk industry was closed. After Gertrude died in 1889, the Society continued with few Harmonists and, in 1905, it dissolved. Old Economy Village still exists and is open to the public. Old Economy Village, Fourteenth and Church Streets, Ambridge, PA 15003.

Sample books in the collection of Old Economy Village reveal that silks were dyed in a wide range of vivid blues, greens, reds, and purples produced from indigo, cochineal, and logwood.
Source: *Piecework*, July/August 1994, p. 42. Photograph © 1993 Deborah Cannarella.

by Quakeress Susannah Wright of Lancaster County in 1770. Silk quilts were also made. One fine example was made by Quakeress Elizabeth Smedley of Philadelphia in 1891 and is now in the collection of the Smithsonian Institution. It displays the simplicity and fine quilting associated with the Amish quilts of Pennsylvania.

The Industrialization of Silk

The change in American society from an agricultural to an industrial base began. The Cheney Brothers started a silk mill in 1838 in Manchester, Connecticut. When the supply of American silk cocoons slowly dried up, the Cheneys began processing raw silk that was imported from Japan. It was brought from Yokohama by the Merchant Marine's express liners to the dock in San Francisco and from there by the "Silk Special" train to New York in less than twenty days. By 1922 there were more than five hundred silk mills and the number of employees in the American silk industry had grown to an impressive one hundred twenty-five thousand. The Cheney firm boasted of keeping many of their employees for more than fifty years. Between the two world wars, the United States processed as much raw silk as all the silk manufacturing countries in Europe taken together. In 1941 this process abruptly stopped when the new synthetics took over.

SILK TODAY

Although cultivating silk caterpillars is still a labor-intensive hand process, production of silk is increasing today because of improvements in productivity and advanced technology. Demand is increasing as well. More than thirty countries are involved in sericulture. China is the largest producer of silk, and the rest of the world is dependent on China for raw silk. India invests a lot in research in order to compete with China. Japan is the largest consumer of silk; whereas at one time it was the largest exporter, it now has to import. Brazil and Korea are important raw silk exporters. European silk mills, at beautiful Lake Como in Italy, Lyon in France, and Spitalsfield and Macclesfield in England, process imported raw silk into exquisite and mostly expensive silk fabrics.

While silk is no longer an imperial prerogative, with the prices, the quantity, and the quality of silk production increasing every year, it is destined to remain a superior, exclusive fabric and it is unlikely ever to become a common commodity. Still, it is within the reach of quilters who wish to infuse their quilts with "wisps of woven wind," the finest textile in the world.

CHAPTER 2

CREATING SILK

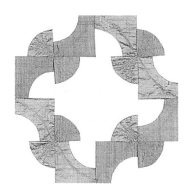

"This was my first silk quilt. The pattern is a simple one, but when rendered in glistening silks, the visual effect is most intriguing."

Drunkard's Path
Hanne Vibeke de Koning-Stapel, 1982. 93" × 93" (236cm × 236cm). Hand pieced, hand quilted. Photograph by Sam Dunlop.

Sericulture has not changed much since it began more than five-thousand years ago. It is the amazing story of how a larva or caterpillar, within a short period of about forty days, converts a vegetable product into a protein fiber—the longest and strongest natural continuous filament in the world. This incredible transformation is part of the mystery of silk, the strongest yet most delicate natural textile.

THE LIFE CYCLE OF THE CULTIVATED SILK MOTH

My journey to discover silk took me to Thailand and China, where I studied silk production. In the region of Korat in northeastern Thailand, I witnessed the entire sericulture process at the huge plant where the Jim Thompson Cooperative produces silk. In China, I visited a rural community in Wuxi, two hundred kilometers west of Shanghai, where farm families have grown mulberry trees and reared silkworms through the ages.

Nurturing the Silkworms

In Wuxi, the leaves of mulberry trees are picked by women who carry heavy loads to feed the greedy little silkworms or caterpillars. Two hundred pounds of mulberry leaves are needed to produce just one pound of raw silk. The eggs laid by the female moth are oval and yellow, less than 0.04″ (1mm) long. They are kept cool until the mulberry trees are budding. Then the eggs, which now look like poppyseeds, are brought to hatch at a temperature of 77°F to 80°F (25°C to 27°C). When they hatch, the caterpillars are dark in color and the size of small ants. They are placed on finely chopped young mulberry leaves in large flat baskets that are stacked on top of each other in the breeding shed or nursery.

White mulberry trees photographed in the parklike landscape of the Jim Thompson plant. Korat, Thailand.

With a ferocious appetite, the caterpillars eat all the leaves. Every three to four hours around the clock, the trays are cleaned and replenished. Temperature and humidity are controlled, kept at optimum levels. Hygiene is taken very seriously because silkworms are super-sensitive to irregularities, noises, and smells. It is obvious that this labor-intensive process can take place only where labor is cheap and plentiful.

Baskets of mulberry leaves are brought to the weighing station where the harvest of mulberry leaves is registered. Wuxi, China.

Silkworms spend their early lives in beautiful round and oval baskets made of rice straw. Wuxi, China.

Mulberry leaves are chopped
into small pieces for the newly
hatched silkworms.
Wuxi, China.

Silkworm eggs
Source: Fibo Beeldonderwijs B. V.,
Rotterdam, The Netherlands.

As the caterpillars grow, they are fed whole branches with leaves. In the nursery there is a constant munching sound, which has been compared to the fizz in a glass of Alka Seltzer®. They eat for about thirty-three days, interrupting their meal only when molting. They molt or shed their skins four times, and change to a creamy light color. The fully developed caterpillar has grown from ⅛″ (3mm) to 3¾″ (9cm), and its weight has multiplied more than seven thousand times.

*The worms and chopped leaves
are stacked in large flat
baskets, which are cleaned and
replenished every few hours.*
Wuxi, China.

The fully developed caterpillar
Source: Copyright © S. Nagendra,
The National Audubon Society
Collection/Photo Researchers.

Cocooning

Now the caterpillars are ready to build their cocoons. They are moved by hand either to mats of rice straw, or to celled trays, which are tiny boxes stacked next to and on top of each other. At the silk farm I visited, the caterpillars were put onto brightly colored plastic mats. The caterpillar first spins a few threads between its walls to gain support—best compared to a hammock. Then it spins the outside of the cocoon and, finally, by moving its head in a figure-eight configuration, builds itself completely into the cocoon at an amazing speed. In two to three days, the caterpillar spins a filament of more than two thousand yards (about two thousand meters).

This amazing chemistry takes place in two serific glands inside the caterpillar's body. The filament consists mainly of two ingredients: the fibroin, which is the protein textile fiber, seventy-five percent to eighty percent of the weight; and the sericin, also a protein and a gummy substance, twenty to twenty-five percent of the weight. From each gland

The completed cocoon
Source: Copyright © David M. Schleser, Nature's Images, Inc., The National Audubon Society Collection/Photo Researchers.

The caterpillar changes into a chrysalis.
Source: Fibo Beeldonderwijs B. V., Rotterdam, The Netherlands.

The caterpillars are moved onto mats.
Wuxi, China.

the thread, called a *brin*, is extruded through the spinneret in the caterpillar's lower jaw. The two brins, now called a *bave*, are bonded together and protected by the sericin, which hardens on contact with air. The cocoon now consists of many concentric layers of silk thread, which is porous so the caterpillar can continue to breathe.

When spinning is finished, the caterpillar has emptied itself and changed into a chrysalis, a hard brown shell. Within a week, metamorphosis takes place inside the chrysalis: the creation of a moth. The moth exudes a brown liquid that makes a hole in the cocoon through which the moth climbs out. But when the moth leaves the cocoon through that hole, the filament is broken and is no longer one continuous thread. Therefore, a selection takes place as soon as the spinning is finished: the majority of the cocoons are sorted out and the chrysalides are stifled or killed.

Only the best cocoons are chosen to complete the cycle for procreation. The domesticated moth that climbs out of the cocoon has wings but cannot fly. The female moth attracts a male moth by a sex scent; they mate and then the male moth dies.

The female lays her eggs, very carefully making sure that all eggs lie neatly next to each other. She lays two hundred to five hundred eggs and then dies. The full cycle is complete.

From Cocoon to Yarn

The chrysalides of the selected silk cocoons are stifled by hot air, thus leaving the filament intact for reeling. Then imperfect cocoons are sorted out on a conveyor belt; they will be processed as waste silk.

Sericin is boiled off in the degumming process.
Wuxi, China.

The perfect cocoons are packed in white jute sacks and transported to the filature, a huge factory where the filaments are reeled off the cocoons. The cocoons are dumped into a tank of boiling hot water, which dissolves some of the sericin holding the cocoon together. The yellow cocoons contain carotine in the sericin, which is boiled off in the degumming process. Mechanical brushes loosen and remove the floss, or mass of short fibers, on the outside of the softened cocoons.

Filaments are lightly twisted together.
Wuxi, China.

The beginning of the continuous filament is picked out and, by hand or by machine, six to eight filaments (depending on the desired thread thickness) are reeled and lightly twisted together. The thread is reeled first to small spools, then to larger spools; eventually, the thread is reeled into hanks or skeins. Before the finished skeins leave the factory, the silk filament is taken through many steps of processing and controls.

Now the skeins of raw silk, also called *greige* or *grège* silk, are made ready for export. Raw silk has an attractive luster and brilliance, but due to the sericin, it is still hard to the touch. The color, which varies from bright white to bright yellow, is produced by pigments in the sericin. Later, when the sericin is boiled off, the result is degummed white silk, which is soft and lustrous. Silk yarns are usually exported as raw silk because during transport the sericin protects the filament. Thirteen to sixteen pounds (six to seven kilos) of fresh cocoons are required to produce two to two and a half pounds (one kilo) of raw silk.

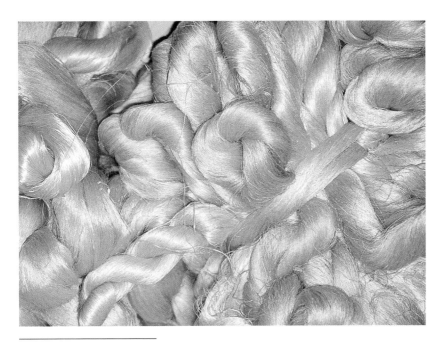

The thread is reeled into hanks or skeins of raw silk.
Wuxi, China.

From Yarn to Fabric

The raw silk filaments are *thrown*, which means they are twisted and doubled together, to produce the necessary strength. Warp yarns must be strong and are twisted more heavily than weft yarns. The yarns are woven into many kinds of fabrics that are degummed before being dyed. However, for iridescent fabrics, the raw silk yarns are first degummed and dyed before they are woven. For exclusive fabrics like damask and brocade, the silk yarns are degummed and dyed before being woven. Yarn dyeing is more expensive than piece or fabric dyeing. (Details on the different weaves and characteristics of various silk fabrics are given in the Glossary.)

It is not possible to reel the fibers of the outer crust or the inner part of the cocoon, but nothing is wasted in sericulture. These floss fibers are carded, combed, and spun like wool. The longer fibers, or *schappe* silk, are woven into spun silk, or used to make silk sewing thread. The shortest fibers, the *noils*, are woven into a fabric called *bourette* or *noil* silk.

Reeling twin cocoons produces doupion silk. When two caterpillars occupy the same cell and spin themselves together in one cocoon, twin cocoons result. One silk authority told me that in twin cocoons it is always a male and a female who are cohabiting (a sericultural romance!). But another silk specialist told me that the sex of the caterpillars is determined only in the chrysalis stage. A special technique is applied to reel twin cocoons, and the filament achieved is uneven, with thick nubs or slubs. Indian and Thai silk weavers especially make use of this irregular thread in the beautiful doupion silks.

Wild Silk Moths

Wild silk and raw silk are two different things. There is common confusion about which is which: raw silk is the product of the cultivated *Bombyx mori* moth, with the sericin still protecting the fibers; wild silk is the product of the semicultivated wild silk moth.

Degummed white silk is soft and lustrous.
Wuxi, China.

Nonmulberry sericulture uses the cocoons of moths that live in jungles on a diet of tropical leaves or, in regions with temperate climates, in forests where they eat oak leaves. Before the Chinese started to domesticate the *Bombyx mori*, families of wild spinning moths were indigenous to China, India, and Japan.

There are many varieties within the Saturnidae family, but their main points of resemblance are their big cocoons, in colors varying from dull white to green to coffee brown, and their ability to fly. The moths and their caterpillars are much bigger than those of the *Bombyx mori*, and the moths are often handsome, with beautiful "eyes" on their wings. However, not all wild cocoons are interesting to quiltmaking silk lovers because the quality and quantity of the thread of some species are poor and unprofitable. Narrators in literature from the seventeenth century talk about "silkplants" because they saw the cocoons hanging from the branches of trees like fruits. The Bengali word for this wild silk is *tasar* or *tussah*.

Of particular interest are the silks of the Japanese *Antheraea yamamai* and the Chinese and Indian tussah moth, the *Antheraea pernyi*. On a diet

Wild cocoons showing attachment to tree branch, circa. 1887
Source: Collection of the Dutch Textile Museum, Tilburg, The Netherlands.

of oak leaves in the cold climate of Manchuria, the wild silk caterpillar makes a coarse and dark thread. When the wild moths live and breed in a mild climate with light soil, as in the Chinese province of Shantung, this same tussah caterpillar produces a silk thread that is lighter in color and weight, the well-known shantung silk.

Wild silk moth
Source: Copyright © Kjell B. Sandved, The National Audubon Society Collection/ Photo Researchers.

Harvesting Wild Cocoons

All wild species are semidomesticated, which means they are cultivated in a wild state: the farmers take care of the environment in which the wild caterpillars live and chase predators away. However, the caterpillars feed themselves and find their own places to build cocoons, and the moths do not lose their ability to fly.

The cocoons of the wild spinners are much larger than those of the *Bombyx mori*. But the wild cocoons are not as compact as those of the cultivated species, and the filament is much shorter, coarser, and irregular. It is extremely difficult, if not impossible, to reel any part of the filament off the cocoons; all fibers are carded and spun, like the waste silk of the *Bombyx mori*.

The sericin has penetrated the silk fibers of the wild cocoons, so it's not entirely removed in the degumming process. This means that the spinners' yarns are harder to the touch and not as brilliant as mulberry silk; they don't absorb dyes as greedily and readily as the *Bombyx mori* silk. Also, they don't drape as well as many of the cultivated silks (a significant deterrent to the makers of garments, but not a detriment to quiltmakers). The wild silks have a charm and beauty of their own, and the smell and appearance of wild silk have their own attraction.

Other wild silks of interest to quilters are the golden-yellow muga of Assam and the white eri of Bengal and Nepal, both from India. Both mulberry silks and wild silks are wonderful to work with in quiltmaking. Pieces of lustrous silk as accents will enrich traditional as well as contemporary quilts. The attractive textures of many wild silks will add interest to any kind of quilt.

Wild silk caterpillar beginning to build a cocoon.
Source: Copyright © J. H. Carmichael, The National Audubon Society Collection/Photo Researchers.

CHAPTER 3

Thai Make Do
Hanne Vibeke de Koning-Stapel, 1994.
62" × 74" (157cm × 185cm). Machine
pieced, hand quilted; antique silk
sarongs from Thailand. Photograph by
Sharon Risedorph.

UNDERSTANDING SILK

Silk, the queen of textiles, owes its reputation to its regal sheen and
luster, to its pleasant feel and drape, and to its tensile strength and
resilience. The lustrous filament yarns have inspired textile artisans through
the ages to invent intricate weaves in which these characteristics are
showcased. Since ancient times, dyers have come up with the most
wonderful colors that penetrate the smooth silk filament, so that silk yarns
and silk fabrics reflect hues in more brilliant depths than any other textile.
In order to exploit the distinguishing features of silk, it is useful to know
something about its properties.

CHEMISTRY AND CHARACTERISTICS OF SILK

Like wool, silk is an animal fiber consisting mainly of insoluble proteins. In
form and structure, the silk fiber is the thinnest of all natural fibers and
also the simplest of all textile fibers. If you inspect a silk fiber of the
Bombyx mori, the cultivated silk moth, under a microscope, you will see
that the fiber consists of two brins, which together look like a flat cylinder,
smooth with long molecules. Each of the two brins is vaguely triangular
and hyaline (transparent). The sericin that cements the brins together is
irregular and rough, and only when the sericin is boiled off does the
triangular form reflect the light like a prism. The luster is most pronounced
in the filament, less so in spun silk, which consists of short, carded and
spun fibers.

Silk is hygroscopic, which means it absorbs and retains moisture from the air. When wet, silk can be stretched and it loses some of its strength. When dry, it regains its shape and strength.

Irregularities in the weaves of many silk fabrics are not faults or flaws. They are inevitable in the process of creating a natural, handmade product. Slubs, lumps, and nubs add to the charm and are part of the character of the fabric.

Mulberry silks are crease resistant when the sericin has been boiled off. Wrinkles can be hung out of quality silk. The tussah spinners produce wild silk in which sericin is part of the thread and impossible to boil off completely, the reason why these silks may crease somewhat.

Joshoku Kaiko Tewaza Gusa (*Women's Work in Silk Culture*) Kitagawa Utamaro, Japan, 1754–1806. Woodblock print of early Japanese silk making, c. 1802. 15″ × 10″ (38.1cm × 25.4cm). Source: The Art Institute of Chicago, Clarence Buckingham Collection of Japanese Prints, obtained with Departmental funds. 1925.3246-57. Photograph © The Art Institute of Chicago, all rights reserved.

In the first of these woodblock prints depicting early Japanese silk making, women brush silkworm eggs from the papers upon which they were laid and put them into hatching boxes.

Women gather mulberry leaves to feed caterpillars.

How to Recognize the Genuine Thing

Even if technology has not been able to chemically imitate the silk protein fiber, you may still come across manmade fibers that look and behave much like silk. If you want to be sure which material you have at hand, try the burn test. Take care as you handle fire for the burn test! It's important to test both warp and weft threads. Pull some threads of each and, keeping them between tweezers (above a sink or other flame-resistant receptacle), set fire to one end and withdraw the fire immediately. Silk will hardly burn with a flame; instead it glows, and a soft blackish residue of ash is left, which crumbles when touched. The smell is vaguely that of burned meat.

The process of chopping mulberry leaves and feeding the pieces to the young caterpillars, repeated five times daily.

Removing the dried pieces of mulberry leaves from the feeding trays with a feather. The women then place the trays upon racks where they are kept at an even temperature while the caterpillars are dormant.

In comparison, polyesters will burn with a quick flame and black smoke, and will leave hardly any residue. Polyesters give off an artificial smell.

Quilt artists Cynthia Morgan of Australia and Yvonne Porcella of the United States both use this burning characteristic of silk to advantage in their quiltmaking. See their work on pages 69 and 91.

The selvage reveals whether the silk is hand or machine woven. If the edge is slightly irregular, it is hand woven; if the selvage is straight, it is machine woven.

Feeding the nearly full-grown caterpillars with whole mulberry leaves.

Examining the newly spun cocoons.

SERICIN AND WEIGHTING

Twenty percent of the weight of mulberry silk consists of the gummy substance called sericin, which protects the fibroin, the protein silk fiber. Because of this protective role, the sericin also impedes absorption of dyestuff. Therefore, before dyeing silk, the sericin must be removed, either from the yarns or from the woven fabric. In this process the yarn or fabric loses twenty percent of its weight, and consequently, twenty percent of its monetary value.

During the second half of the nineteenth century, manufacturers and chemists invented and employed a treatment of silk with metal salts to

Women guide the moths with a thread so that they will lay their eggs on sheets of paper.

Women watch the moths fly away after they have laid their eggs.

compensate for the weight loss. This is called *weighting*. The concept is that the metal salt invades the silk fiber, which swells and gains weight and volume, with the result that the fiber eventually bursts. Weighted silk is sometimes vividly described as dynamited silk.

The heavier the weighting, the shorter the life of the silk. *Weighting a pari* means that after the sericin is removed the weight loss is compensated one hundred percent. *Under pari* means that the weight loss is not completely compensated; *above pari* means that so much metal salt is added that the compensation of the weight loss is above one hundred percent. Sometimes a manufacturer added weight of more than two hundred percent, which to me seems fraudulent.

Women boil the cocoons and reel off the filament of silk.

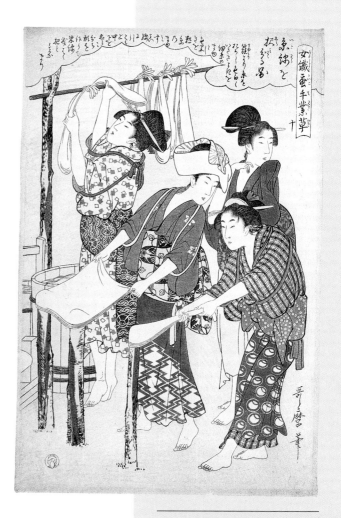

Women dry the coarse outer winding from the cocoons and make it into sheets of mawata, *or floss silk.*

If a silk fabric creases badly, I would not buy it because this may be a warning that the fabric has been treated with a wrong material, maybe a metal salt, resulting in an inferior product.

Silks from the Victorian period (approximately 1850 to 1900) were heavily weighted, and the sad result is that most of the charming crazy quilts from that era have disintegrated. Averil Colby observes that they are "tattered wrecks." Important to us today is the assurance from "inside" silk people that the odious metal salt weighting practice has been totally abandoned, with one or two exceptions: many silks used for men's ties are still metal weighted to give the tie the required stiffness. And the thin organza fabric that is used for elegant haute couture dresses may also be weighted.

The grading and spinning of the silk.

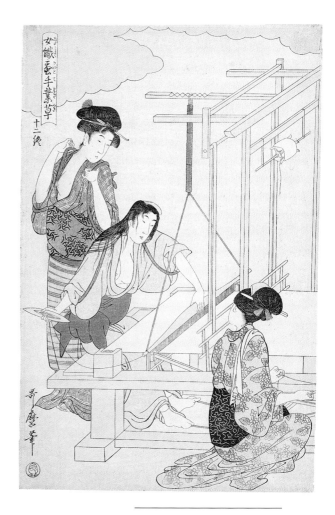

Women weave cloth from the silk.

Samples of Silk Weaves

Several samples are shown here, all dyed in the same blue dye bath, steam fixated. You can see that various weaves take the color differently. The larger swatches are the "right" sides of the fabrics; the smaller swatches are the "wrong" sides, or backs. Some look the same front and back; others are quite different.

Look carefully at the differences between the fronts and backs of the wild silks: shantung, ottoman, tussah natural, and tussah bleached. Then

Weaves of wild silk, front and back.

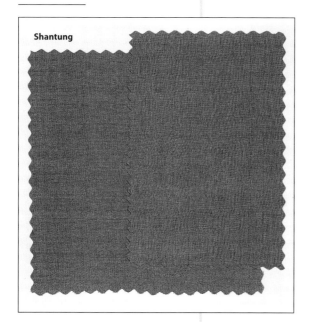

Shantung

Ottoman

Tussah natural

Tussah bleached

note the differences in the cultivated silks: twill, satin/charmeuse, crepe matelassé, and Jacquard crepe cloqué.

Several of the names of silks originate in the French language because France was and still is one of the most important silk-producing countries on the European continent. French weavers created countless new weaves and patterns that were adopted into the silk vocabularies of countries around the world. See the Glossary for definitions of such terms as cloqué, embossing, faconné, and matelassé.

Weaves of cultivated silk, front and back.

Twill

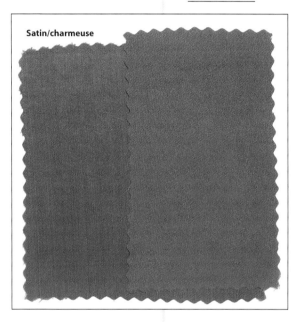

Satin/charmeuse

Crepe matelassé

Jacquard crepe cloqué

In weaving, two important elements are the warp and the weft. The warp refers to the lengthwise yarns which are fastened at even tension to the beams of the loom. These yarns run parallel to each other. The weft refers to the crosswise or filling yarns which are put onto a pirn, which is put into the shuttle. The shuttle is thrown at high speed between the lowered and raised warp yarns, thereby interlacing the two kinds of yarn.

There are various kinds of weaves. The five most common weaves are:

1. **Plain weave.** One weft yarn goes over and under one warp yarn. The front and back look the same if the thickness of both yarns are fairly equal. Fabrics like habutai or pongee, Thai silk, Indian doupion, crepe, taffeta, and organza are all plain weaves. In Great Britain, plain weave is known as tabby weave; in France, it is known as taffeta or toile.

2. **Rib weave.** This is a variation of plain weave, except that a heavy, more prominent yarn is used in the weft and a much thinner yarn in the warp, or vice versa. The ribs or cords are formed by the heavy yarns which conceal the thin yarns. Seam slippage or unravelling may occur parallel to the prominent yarns. Ottoman and faille silks are rib weaves.

Early warping mill
Encyclopédie Diderot et D'Alembert, l'Art de la Soie, Planche XXXVIII.
Source: Collection of the Dutch Textile Museum, Tilburg, The Netherlands.

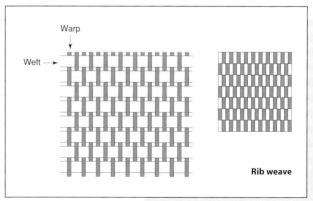

Rib weave

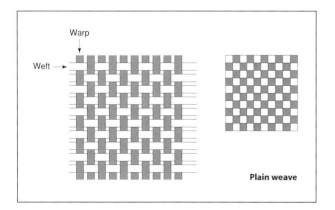

Plain weave

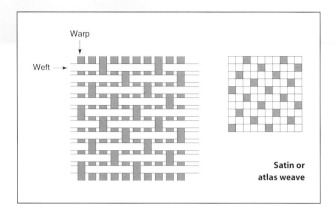

Satin or
atlas weave

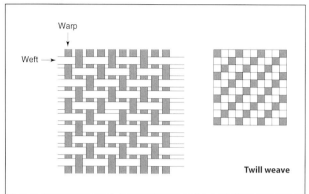

Twill weave

3. **Satin or atlas weave.** Each warp yarn floats over
   several weft yarns. This produces a smooth and shiny
   surface that is vulnerable to snagging by rough objects
   or harsh treatment. The back may have different looks; it is often
   crepy. Satins and charmeuses are satin or atlas weave fabrics.

4. **Twill weave.** Each weft yarn jumps several warp yarns, creating
   diagonal ribs. Twill weave makes a strong fabric. The ribs on the
   right side read from lower left to upper right. Silk twills and
   gabardine are fabrics with diagonal ribs. Twill weaves are known
   as serges in France.

5. **Jacquard weave.** Around 1803, Joseph-Marie Jacquard of Lyon,
   France, invented the loom with punched pattern cards that carries
   his name. Intricate reversible patterns are woven in combination
   with plain, twill, and satin weaves. Elegant fabrics with overlaying
   and underlaying patterns are achieved. The back side of the fabric
   is the negative of the front side. Damask and brocade are woven
   on Jacquard looms.

*17th Century
Chinese draw loom*
Source: Bibliothèque
nationale de France,
Paris, France.

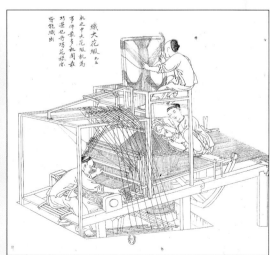

*Métier à Tisser, draw loom with
punched cards as invented by Joseph-
Marie Jacquard in Lyon, France,
around 1803. With the invention of
these punched cards, the French could
produce intricate damask weaves
without the draw boys on top of the
loom, a feature invented and used for
centuries by the Chinese.*
Source: Musée des Tissus, Lyon, France.
Photograph by Pierre Verrier.

In spite of the assurance that weighting with metal salts is not done anymore, you may want to prove this by doing another burn test: hold a small piece of fabric between tweezers and proceed as previously described on page 33. If the ashes show a framelike residue, your silk has probably been weighted. I would not use it—certainly not in a quilt!—because it will not live a long life.

DYEING AND PAINTING

The sericin is boiled off by soaking silk—either the yarns or the woven fabric—in a hot alkaline bath for several hours. When most of the sericin is removed, the smooth surface of the mulberry silk fiber

absorbs dye better than any other fiber. The fibers consist of prisms that catch light and dye pigments in depth. This is especially the case in filament silk, where the prisms are not interrupted. In spun silk, many of these prisms are broken; therefore, spun silk is less lustrous and shimmering than filament silk.

Many quiltmakers dye their own silk fabrics and achieve excellent results. The art of silk dyeing and painting has been part of tradition in China and Japan for more than two thousand years. Following the invention of aniline dyes around 1860, a lot of technical research and development in the chemistry of dyes took place, greatly benefitting quilters today. Using simple methods, it is possible for beginners to achieve splendid results with brilliant and deep colors that may be more colorfast than industrially dyed silks. One of the many rewarding things about silk painting or dyeing is that a huge variety of textures and structures in silk fabrics react to the dyestuff in very different ways. The most surprising results occur when a couple of colors are applied to a piece of silk, or when you put silks of various textures into the same dye bath!

The excellent dye absorption quality of silk also means that more dyestuff may be absorbed than can be retained when washed. It is prudent to test colorfastness by moistening a small piece of the dyed silk; then place it on a piece of white muslin and iron with a warm iron. If the muslin does not color, it should be safe to wash the silk.

There are various techniques to choose from: immersion dyeing, painting on stretched fabric, painting on loose fabric, over-dyeing, and spraying. Many books in several languages have been written on this subject, and silk painting workshops are widely offered. Some good books are listed in the Bibliography.

Yarn-Dyeing or Piece-Dyeing

In the silk industry, there are two ways of dyeing silk fabrics: yarn dyeing, in which the yarns are degummed before dyeing; and piece dyeing, in which the fabric is woven from raw silk with the sericin still present, then degummed before dyeing.

Usually, expensive fabrics are yarn-dyed, which is the more elaborate process. Yarn-dyeing is obviously used for plaids. Shot or iridescent (changeant) silk, in which the weft has a different color from the warp, and also ikats, in which the warp and/or the weft are tie-dyed before weaving, require yarn-dyeing.

Unfortunately, industrially dyed fabrics—cottons and silks alike—are not always colorfast. I know some cases of frustrating disappointments. Over-dyeing may sometimes solve this problem.

The rewards of quiltmaking with silks are, however, much more prominent than the disappointments. With its numerous positive qualities, silk is an excellent material to integrate into both traditional and art quilts.

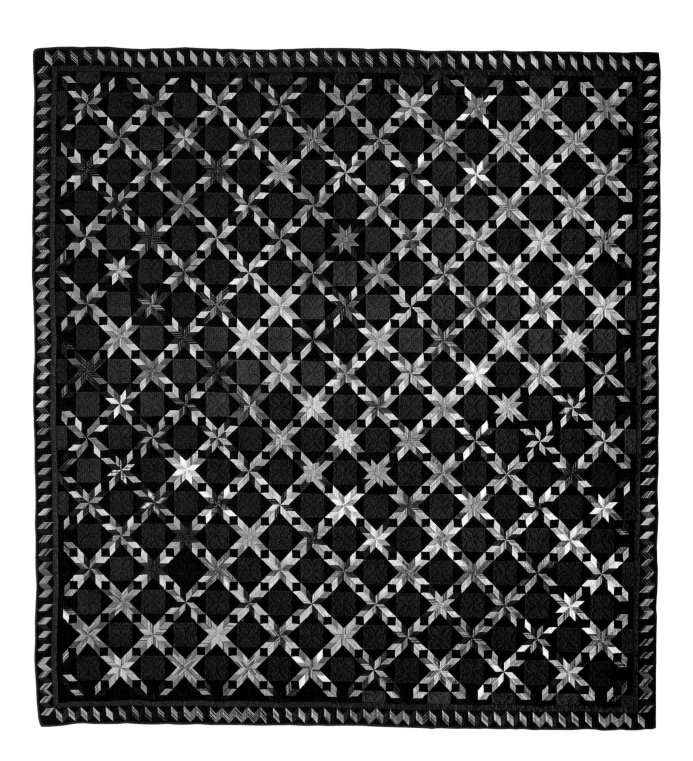

CHAPTER 4

SILK QUILTS THROUGH THE AGES

"A friend brought back from India small lengths of striped and plaid silk fabrics in many colors and challenged me to make a quilt. I combined black crepe de chine and hand-dyed purple Jacquard silk with the Indian fabrics. The stack of arrow blocks just grew and grew—there were enough for a king-size quilt. The pattern was inspired by a quilt from 1860 by an unknown quilt-maker, pictured in American Quilts and Coverlets, *a publication by the Metropolitan Museum of Art, New York.*

Polyhymnia
Hanne Vibeke de Koning-Stapel, 1996. 92½″ × 88″ (235cm × 224cm). Machine and hand pieced by Hanne Vibeke de Koning-Stapel, hand quilted by Gayle P. Ropp, Virginia, U.S.A.; Indian silk plaids, hand-dyed Jacquard and crepe de chine, pongee, Indian doupion. Photograph by Sharon Risedorph.

The English emigrants who left Leiden on the *Mayflower* in 1620, as well as other European pioneers who later crossed the Atlantic Ocean, carried the age-old tradition of patchwork and quilting to the American continent, where this craft developed into a high form of artistic expression. Over time, while interest in quiltmaking waned in Europe, quilts became an American passion. Paradoxically, in recent decades the American patchwork tradition has traveled to Europe, inspiring a new age in European quiltmaking.

EARLY SILK QUILTS IN EUROPE

It may be less well known that the practice of making and using quilts was manifest in several European and Asian countries before and after the voyage of the *Mayflower*. In inventories from the Middle Ages, references to silk quilts are made regularly, but none of these quilts are thought to have survived.

Dutch textile expert An Moonen, in her book on old Dutch quilts, *'t is al Beddegoet, Nederlandse Antieke Quilts 1650–1900*, mentions that Karel V, the Hapsburg emperor whose territory spanned Austria, the Iberian Peninsula, and the Low Countries, gave a silk quilt to his court physician in 1544. This quilt survives and is shown here: crimson red silk, embroidered with silk thread in many colors, with a filling of cotton and a yellow silk

45

fringe, it measures 74″ × 110″ (187cm × 280cm). A double-headed eagle is featured in the center of the medallion, surrounded by narrow borders with fish. In each corner a bird of paradise exhibits lavish tail feathers. The borders display flower and plant ornaments and hunting horsemen, dressed in the costumes of the day. This extraordinary quilt, privately owned in Belgium, is in remarkably good condition for a quilt made more than four hundred fifty years ago.

Karel V's quilt
1544. Silk embroidery on crimson silk. Source: Private collection, Belgium.

In 1540, twenty-three quilts of closely stitched sarcenet were presented to Katherine Howard, one of the wives of King Henry VIII of England. Sarcenet is a plain weave silk, probably first woven by the Spanish Saracens. Another inventory from the British Isles, dated 1584, lists the possessions of Robert Dudley, Earl of Leicester, including several elaborate quilts. One is described as ". . . a faire quilte of crymson sattin . . . , fringed rounde aboute with a small fringe of crymson silke . . . ."

Permanently exhibited in the Rijksmuseum, Amsterdam, are two delightful dollhouses made in the second part of the seventeenth century for two ladies of the well-to-do bourgeoisie. The houses are elaborately furnished and decorated in period fashion, and several beds are covered with silk quilts.

Osier cradle with padded silk quilt from the lying-in room in the Amsterdam dollhouse of Petronella Dunois (1650–1695)
The height of the cradle is 3½″ (9cm). Source: Rijksmuseum, Amsterdam, The Netherlands.

Over the years since my passion for silk began, I have searched out early silk quilts. In the National Museum of Ireland in Dublin, I found an early coverlet made by Florence Giles of Youghal, County Cork. The museum description states that the coverlet was "Embroidered with coloured silks in chain, satin, long and short stitches, quilted ground work in back stitch." The coverlet is dated 1708.

I also came across several silk quilts in the collection of the Victoria and Albert Museum in London, England. This medallion-style quilt with an hourglass pattern and broad borders was created in approximately 1770, possibly by Miss Mary Parker of Crediton for her marriage. It is composed of two and a half inch squares, each made of four triangles. The quilt contains various damasks and striped and watered silks, but the majority of the triangles are made out of ribbons applied to pieces of silk in matching colors. It exhibits an amazing collection of early-eighteenth-century patterned and plain silk ribbons from England and France. Some of the ribbons are woven with metal thread, and

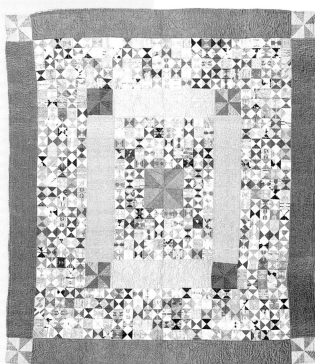

some have a crown pattern, suggesting a royal wedding or coronation. The black silks have disintegrated, showing papers beneath. The rest of the colors are still fresh, and the quilt as a whole is in good condition.

Eastern Influence on Early European Silk Quilts

Two achievements during the Middle Ages made the Far East more accessible to European tradespeople. Marco Polo traveled from Venice to India and China by land—he knew the network of the Silk Route. Portuguese explorer Vasco da Gama discovered the sea route round the African Cape of Good Hope to the Far East. Portuguese colonists started trading posts in India; among the commissioned commodities they brought to the West through Goa were cotton, linen, and silk quilts with silk embroidery made by accomplished needleworkers in Bengal and Cambay, India.

The Saltonstall Quilt

When I first heard of the 1704 Saltonstall patchwork quilt, I was excited; I saw it as evidence that not all silks are so fragile that a silk quilt will perish within one or two generations. Quiltmakers today know that this has been the sad fate of many Victorian quilts because they were made of metal-weighted silks and taffetas in vogue for dresses during the Victorian period (1850–1900). The Saltonstall quilt is now thought to have been of a later date.

The Saltonstall quilt, c. 1704
75″ × 82″ (190.5cm × 208cm). Pieced silk and velvet.
Source: Peabody Essex Museum, Salem, Massachusetts,
U.S.A. Photograph by Mark Sexton. Neg no. 17,658.

Portuguese silk quilt
Seventeenth century. 102″ × 77″ (259cm × 195cm). Embroidered silk quilt made of wild silk, chain stitch embroidery with silk thread. Source: Museu Nacional de Arte Antiga, Lisbon, Portugal. Photograph by Divisão de Documentãção Fotográfica, Instituto Português de Museus.

An Indo-Portuguese quilt from the early seventeenth century survives, made of yellow silk, richly embroidered with many colors of silk thread. The center of the quilt shows two birds facing each other with a crown above them. In the borders there are profuse floral motifs and in the corners Hindu mythological figures appear.

The Portuguese brought emblem books to the Indo-Portuguese colonies; these picture books were popular and influential when bookprinting was still at a young age. From these picture books native designers drew their artistic impressions on fabric, and needleworkers executed them in thread. These quilts were very costly and were commissioned and used as bedquilts by wealthy people in Portugal. Written observations and inventories from that period prove that the production of these quilts must have been abundant. Today, a number of them are part of the textile collections in several museums in the United States and Europe; unfortunately, they are rarely shown to the public.

Dutch Eastern Trade

The Dutch were next to colonize the Far East, where they became rivals to the Portuguese by starting their own trading posts. Pepper, nutmeg, and cinnamon were desirable import trade goods,

Chintz quilt with silk backing
Friesland, 1700–1725. 87″ × 124″ (220cm × 313cm). Hand quilted with silk thread. Source: Netherlands Open-Air Museum, National Heritage Museum, Arnhem, the Netherlands. Photograph by Frans van Ameijde.

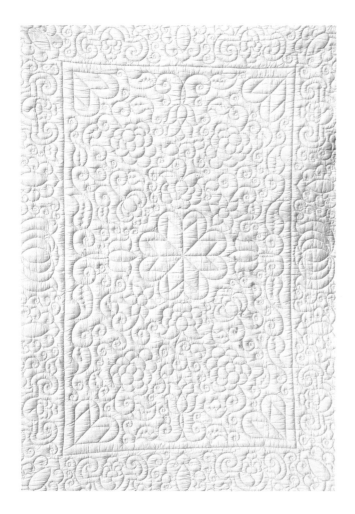

but almost one third of their trade consisted of textiles—silks and cotton chintzes.

The Dutch imported quilts from India, but the Dutch taste was completely different from that of the Portuguese; the quilts exported to the Netherlands in the seventeenth and eighteenth centuries were made of painted or printed cotton chintzes with silk backings. A huge piece, the Friesland quilt, dating from 1700 to 1725, comes from the Coromandelcoast and is quilted from the side of the greenish silk backing. In this kind of quilt, the stitching sometimes follows the pattern of the chintz, which gives a rather messy impression on the back. Here, however, the quilting pattern is quite beautiful.

A wonderful cream-colored satin crib quilt was found by a friend in an antique store in Haarlem, Holland. The fabric is the softest silk I have ever had between my fingers. (The store owner's cat must have felt the same because it was sleeping on the quilt in the sunny store window.) Amazingly, my friend paid very little for this unusual beauty. It has four layers and was hand quilted with silk thread in Holland around 1710 to 1725 in an ornamental pattern typical of that period. The tiny quilting stitches go through a thin woven woolen blanket and some carded cotton fibers. The back is loose, fastened to the quilt top only along the edges of all four sides.

Crib quilt
Anonymous, the Netherlands, c. 1725. 42½″ × 49½″ (108cm × 126cm). Source: Josje van Duyneveldt, the Netherlands. Photograph by Sharon Risedorph.

Three Dutch Treasures

Cream satin silk quilt
Quilter unknown, 1650–1700.
54″ × 85″ (137cm × 215cm).
Quilted and embroidered.
Source: Kasteel Middachten,
de Steeg, the Netherlands.
Photograph by Frans van
Ameijde. Originally published
in *'t is al Beddegoet* by An
Moonen, Terra Publishing,
Holland, 1996.

The castle Middachten in eastern Holland has been in the same family for centuries. Among this family's treasures are three silk quilts that are all still in use! The first is from 1650 to 1700; although the cream silk fabric of the front is worn, this quilt is exhibited once in a while at the castle. It has both lavish embroidery and quilting through all three layers. The middle layer is carded wool and the back is coarse woven wool.

The second quilt, circa 1750, is reversible with front and back made of green satin silk and a filling of carded cotton. The floral quilt pattern is similar to the quilt patterns used in petticoats of that period. This quilt was probably made by a professional quilter in Holland. The floral motif is enhanced by fine lines of background quilting.

The third quilt, a patchwork coverlet with a medallion, has a green silk back and no filling. It was made by Countess Bentinck, who spent part of her life in the castle. The coverlet was made around 1845 of many kinds of silk: various damasks, satins, and crepes from the eighteenth and nineteenth centuries. The oldest silks, from the 1700s, are still in perfect condition, whereas more recent silks from the 1800s are worn because they were weighted with metal salts.

Child's quilt
Quilter unknown, c. 1750.
34″ × 39½″ (86cm × 110cm).
Green satin silk on both sides.
Source: Kasteel Middachten,
de Steeg, the Netherlands.
Also published in *'t is al
Beddegoet*, An Moonen, Terra
Publishing, Holland, 1996.
Photograph by Frans van
Ameijde.

Silk coverlet
Countess Caroline Mechtild
Bentinck van Waldeck Pyrmont,
c. 1845. 79″ × 90″ (200cm ×
253cm). Damasks, satins, crepes,
and other silks from eighteenth
and nineteenth centuries.
Source: Kasteel Middachten, de
Steeg, the Netherlands. Also
published in *'t is al Beddegoet*,
An Moonen, Terra Publishing,
Holland, 1996. Photograph by
Frans van Ameijde.

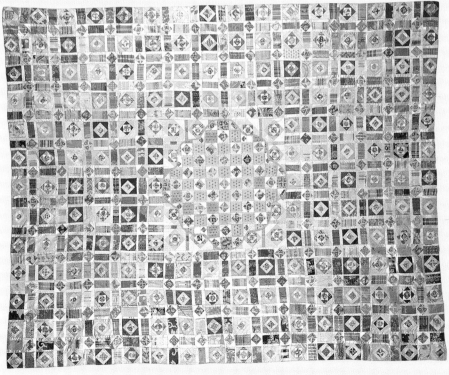

Quilted silk petticoats or skirts were fashionable in the United States and Europe during most of the eighteenth century. A yellow silk satin petticoat, now part of the collection of the Netherlands Open-Air Museum, Arnhem, Holland, richly quilted with intricate floral motifs, was professionally made in the Netherlands around 1775 and is in perfect condition. The filling is carded wool and the back is linen.

When these beautiful pieces of clothing went out of fashion around 1800, they were often made into quilts by cutting the width in two halves and sewing them together. Shown is an elaborately embroidered and quilted example of this kind of quilt; the horizontal seam in the middle is visible. The back is a hand-painted chintz made between 1775 and 1800 in India.

Quilted silk petticoat
Probably made by a professional quilter, c. 1775. Source: Netherlands Open-Air Museum, National Heritage Museum, Arnhem, Holland. Photograph by Martin Wijdemans.

Quilt made from a quilted and embroidered petticoat
Quilter unknown, c. 1750–1800. 65″ × 89″ (165cm × 225cm). Source: An Moonen, Westervoort, the Netherlands. Original publication: An Moonen, *'t is al Beddegoet*, Terra Publishing, Holland, 1996. Photograph by Frans van Ameijde.

The southern part of France, Provence, with its busy port of trade, Marseilles, was a melting pot of many cultures from the Mediterranean basin since the early Middle Ages. In the fertile environments of rich nobility and bourgeoisie, needle arts and crafts reached expert quality, not only in individual households for personal use, but also in professional ateliers or workshops, where needleworkers made a living sewing hand-quilted pieces of garments, such as petticoats, skirts, jackets, and vests for export. Whole-cloth quilts were made of imported cotton, but also of silk fabrics, either home-grown in the Cévennes and Lyon or imported from Italy. This coverlet was meant to cover the feet and ankles of a reclining woman. The front is salmon-colored taffeta silk. The back is also a light silk fabric. The motif is a family coat of arms. Characteristic of quilts from Marseilles in the seventeenth and eighteenth centuries is the use of a filling of silk floss fibers, deriving from the outside of the silk cocoon. This makes the coverlet extremely light. Compare this to the Provençal quilt shown next, which is at least six times as heavy because of the carded cotton filling.

Couvre Pieds Matelassé, quilted foot coverlet, mid-eighteenth century
53½″ × 66″ (138cm × 168cm). Collection of Mme Marie-José Eymar-Beaumelle, Antique Textiles Expert, Marseilles, France.

Provence silk quilt
Quilter unknown, c. 1860.
62½″ × 62½″
(158cm × 158cm).
Hand quilted; iridescent silks, filling of very thick carded cotton fibers. Source: Collection of Hanne Vibeke de Koning-Stapel.

Northern European Quilts

In the northeastern corner of Europe, in
Sweden, silk quilts are part of the textile collections in many museums. In Kalmar Läns
Museum, on the southern Baltic coast, I saw
various kinds, all made in Sweden. Alas, as in so
many similar cases, the quilt is there, but documentation is lacking. One fine example is a
yellow satin silk quilt with a rectangular blue and
white medallion embroidered and quilted in silk
thread. The corners display rich embroidery.
The quilting is done in a running stitch with
double lines. The year 1796 is embroidered on
the back of the quilt. It was the property of a
well-to-do family from one of the manor houses
near Kalmar, and it is in perfect condition.

In Sweden, when a marriage was
announced, it was customary for the mother of the bride or the bride's
girlfriends to make a bridal quilt, which was often done in silk. Also in
Kalmar Läns Museum is an extremely beautiful example of white silk,
richly quilted in very fine stitches and made in 1840.

*Yellow damask silk quilt from
Kölby Estate, south of Kalmar,
Sweden*
Quilter unknown, quilt dated
1796 on the back of the quilt in
yellow silk thread on a blue
ribbon. 86″ × 86″
(221cm × 221cm). Source:
Kalmar Läns Museum, Sweden.
Photograph by Rolf Lind.

Brudtäcke, *or marriage quilt*
Quilter unknown, 1840. 85″ ×
89″ (215cm × 225cm). Source:
Kalmar Läns Museum, Sweden.
Photograph by Rolf Lind.

Anders Berch, who lived in Sweden in the 1700s, documented silk fabrics characteristic at that time, such as silk damasks, satins, tabbies, and mantua. We know that silk fabrics were made in Sweden, but according to Berch some were imported from England.

SILK QUILTS IN THE NEW WORLD

Inventories in Great Britain document that quilts were made, often professionally, and when they were made of silk they were destined for the households of well-to-do people. In Anglo-Irish poet and novelist Jonathan Swift's narrative *Gulliver's Travels*, Gulliver describes the clothes that the Lilliputians made for him: they looked like the patchwork made by the ladies in England. This novel was written in 1726, the same year that a wonderful patchwork silk coverlet was made. The year is appliquéd on it. This coverlet is now part of the collection of the McCord Museum, Montreal, Canada. Textile curator Jacqueline Beaudoin-Ross presumes that

The McCord coverlet
Quilter unknown, 1726.
78″ × 82″ (197cm × 207cm). Source: McCord Museum of Canadian History, Montreal, Canada.

Bedcover
England, c. 1730. 93″ × 65″
(236cm × 165cm). Appliqué
and couching. Source: National
Museum of American History,
The Smithsonian Institution,
Washington D.C., U.S.A.
#89.10658 T.1985.0154.

it is of English origin and, in a study of the quilt, comes to the conclusion
that "the McCord quilt's construction, design, and fabrics all clearly
indicate that its appliquéd date relates directly to the period of its execu-
tion." She goes on to say, "There is written evidence that silk quilts, probably of the whole-cloth variety, were present in New France during the
early eighteenth century, being located in centers such as Montreal,
Quebec City, and the Fortress of Louisbourg."

The center medallion of the McCord quilt is a personal interpretation
of the eight-pointed star; the spaces between the starpoints are filled with
patchwork. Between the medallion and the wide border of multicolored
English or Dutch brocaded green silk are rows of *Yankee Puzzle* blocks,
pieced over paper templates. Except for a few pieces of cotton and linen,
silks of various types have been used: damask, brocade, embroidered silks,
and velvets. The backing is early eighteenth century striped silk. It is not
quilted.

Antique silk quilts are prized possessions in many American quilt
museums. Notable among them are the silk quilts in the Smithsonian
Institution's collection in Washington, D.C. One of the earliest, made in
approximately 1730, is a dark-blue satin silk quilt, profusely appliquéd and
embroidered with Persian-style scrollwork and flowers of colored silks. Fine
white and yellow cording covers the edges of all the motifs. The maker of
this lovely piece is unknown, but its provenance may have been England.

Large star shapes made of tiny 1⅜″ (3.5cm) hexagons were carefully pieced in a mid-nineteenth century quilt by an anonymous quiltmaker. Of special interest is a second, probably earlier, red silk quilt used as a second lining. The two complete quilts are stitched together around the edges and finished with green binding. A machine-pleated red silk ribbon is attached to the edges of the red silk quilt.

Pieced quilt

Mid-nineteenth century. 73½″ × 65⅜″ (187cm × 166cm). Hexagons, pieced. Source: National Museum of American History, The Smithsonian Institution, Washington D.C., U.S.A. #95.7187 T. 12917.

A Tumbling Blocks quilt, made in approximately 1880 by Mrs. Harriet Fry Hockaday of Lathrop, Clinton County, Missouri, displays a variety of silk fabrics and textures. Hexagonal blocks fashioned from green, butterscotch, and salmon silks are set with black silk triangles. Dark-red silk velvet hexagons appear in the center of each block. The black silk center and four corners feature floral silk embroidery. The quilt is lined with a second quilt, made of lavender-blue silk with a magenta silk border.

Mary Hise was born in 1797 and lived until 1878. In 1813, she married William Norton, and moved from Pennsylvania to her new home in Russellville, Kentucky. Here, during the second quarter of the nineteenth century, she made a Blazing Star quilt comprised of thirty-six silk stars. The stars are set with green silk squares and rectangles, and the quilt is bound with blue silk. A detail shows the rich quilting and elaborate stuffing.

The Quaker quilt shown on page 16 (detail at left) is thought to be pieced by Elizabeth Smedley of Philadelphia for the trousseau of Elizabeth Webster Smedley before her marriage to Walter Brinton of Philadelphia in 1891. The quilt is made of alternating bands of brown satin silk and tan checked silk, with a brown satin silk border.

It may come as a surprise to quilters today that the American quiltmaking tradition includes quite a number of exquisite silk quilts. Silk was produced in the old colonies prior to and after the Revolutionary War, but always in limited quantities and at high cost. Therefore, similar to silks used in dressmaking, I think that silk fabric was used only in best quilts that were considered show pieces. They were treated with special care and handed down within the family for generations. It is notable that the silk quilts bequeathed to museums often have documentation of the maker and provenance.

SILK PATCHWORK FROM THE FAR EAST

Buddhism traveled from India to China by the Silk Road network. Buddha was born in India as Prince Siddhartha in the sixth century B.C. Raised in luxury and protected from the miseries of the world, when he finally came into contact with human suffering he abandoned his privileged life, went to live and meditate as an ascetic in the forest, and dressed in the discarded clothing of lay people.

Buddha's disciples lived in poverty; out of reverence, lay people offered pieces of valuable silks to these monks, who made simple patchwork dresses. By the time Buddhism came to Korea and China in the first century A.D., these dresses had developed into ritual garments called *kesa*, which were and still are of great significance in the practice of Buddhism, as symbols of Buddhist teaching.

Centuries-old rules and traditions are observed when sewing patches together for *kesa*. These robes are mostly made of rich silks and built up in columns. There are three types: the five-column, the seven-column, and the nine- to twenty-five column *kesa*. Within each column are squares and rectangles in numbers and measurements according to strict rules. The number of columns indicates the importance of the monk or the ceremony for which the *kesa* is made.

Further development of *kesa* as the robes of Buddhist monks took place when Buddhism came to Japan in the sixth century A.D. The convergence of sacred and secular garments has had a tremendous, positive influence on the development of Japanese textile arts, including the art of producing silk fabrics. There are many extant examples of Japanese silk *kesa* in Western museums, especially in the United States.

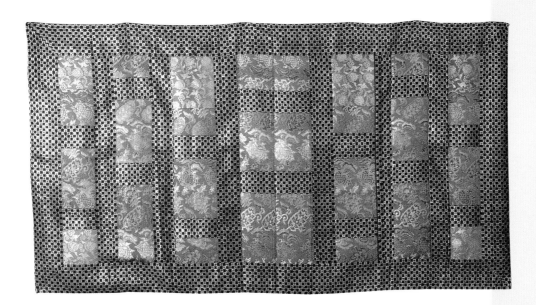

***Seven-column* kesa**
End of the eighteenth or beginning of the nineteenth century, Japan. 80½″ × 43″ (204cm × 110cm). Silk in checkerboard weave and brocade with gold and silver paper lamellae. Source: Association pour l'Etude et la Documentation des Textiles D'Asie, Paris, France, #1629. Photograph by Mathieu Ravaux, R.M.N.

***Nine-column* kesa**
Nineteenth century, Japan. 79½″ × 48½″ (201cm × 123cm). Silk moiré gauze with polychrome and gold embroidery of cranes (symbol of longevity) and skies; probably a summer *kesa*. Source: Association pour l'Etude et la Documentation des Textiles D'Asie, Paris, France, #1497A. Photograph by Mathieu Ravaux, R.M.N.

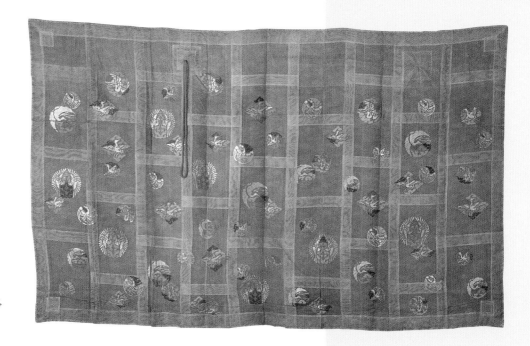

Pojagi *in Korea*

In the Far East we find beautiful patchwork, now part of Korean culture, with a totally different purpose and tradition than *kesa*. From ancient times, caring for silkworms, spinning silk thread, weaving cloth, sewing, and embroidery were the daily tasks of Korean women, who were not allowed to participate in men's intellectual and political lives; they were obedient servants, living in their own separate quarters. Their outlet was creativity with needle and thread, making beautiful silk dresses and costumes, and also *pojagi*, or wrapping cloths,

Norigae Po
Nineteenth century. 16″ × 16″ (41cm × 41cm). Wrapping cloth, hand pieced; satin weave silk. The Chinese characters in the borders talk about "double happiness" and "longevity."
Source: The Museum of Korean Embroidery, Seoul, Korea.

Oppo
Nineteenth century. 37½″ × 37½″ (95cm × 95cm). Hand pieced; fifteen different self-patterned silks and taffetas.
Source: The Museum of Korean Embroidery, Seoul, Korea.

Sang Po
Nineteenth century. 12½″ × 12″ (47cm × 46cm). Silk with self-patterned design. Source: The Museum of Korean Embroidery, Seoul, Korea.

used for many purposes in every household. *Pojagi* cloths were pieces of art, either embroidered or made in patchwork, mostly of silk or ramie, a fabric woven of a flax-like fiber. *Pojagi* were integrated into the lives of all classes in Korea, and were used not only for wrapping, but also for covering food and ceremonial objects. The *Sang Po* shown here is a cloth to cover food on a tray or table, with a loop to lift it. The food was prepared in the women's quarters and carried to the men's quarters, covered with a *Sang Po*. This patchwork cloth is tufted; others have tiny, decorative embroidered bat-knots to keep the top and lining together. The *Norigae Po* is a wrapping cloth for small personal ornaments. The *Oppo* is a wrapping cloth for clothing.

Nomadic Patchwork in Uzbekistan

Nomads in Uzbekistan (Uzbek Republic) decorated the bags in which they carried their belongings with beautiful patchwork, often done in locally produced ikat silk. When these nomadic people of Turkish origin settled into permanent adobe houses at the end of the nineteenth century, they used these patchwork pieces as wall hangings. The Uzbek people are masters in producing silk ikat fabric, which is widely used in both men's and women's garments.

From early times, textiles have primarily been used to cover body, bed, or food. The gallery of embroidered quilts, patchwork quilts, whole-cloth quilts, monks' patchwork robes, and patchwork wrapping cloths in this chapter has taken us to places all over the world and through several centuries. In the next chapter, I'll take you on a journey to places where I discovered contemporary silk quilts and quilting silkaholics like myself.

Patchwork wall hanging
Uzbekistan, end of nineteenth century. 31″ × 29¼″ (78cm × 74cm). Silk ikat. Source: Linden-Museum Stuttgart, Stuttgart, Germany.

CHAPTER 5

A GALLERY OF CONTEMPORARY SILK QUILTS

"My daughter and son-in-law wanted a large quilt for their bedroom. The chintz curtains with big burgundy flowers and blue and green leaves were the starting point for the stars in this quilt."

Stella Florealis
Hanne Vibeke de Koning-Stapel, 1996. 96″ × 96″ (244cm × 244cm). Machine pieced, hand quilted; Indian doupion, satin, Thai silk, cotton chintz. Photograph by Sharon Risedorph.

In 1971, Jonathan Holstein and Gail van der Hoof presented part of their collection in a major exhibition of American quilts as a design tradition. These mostly Amish quilts from 1860 to 1940 raised quiltmaking above the designation of folk art to that of graphic art in many viewers' eyes. The premiere took place in the Whitney Museum of American Art in New York, after which this important exhibition traveled to several museums in the United States. The revival of quiltmaking in the United States had begun.

TRADITIONAL QUILTS AND ART QUILTS AROUND THE WORLD

The Holstein and van der Hoof exhibition also made its way to Europe, where it toured museums in various countries, releasing and stimulating creativity in countless viewers. An important consequence was that in the 1970s European women started making patchwork quilts. In France and Germany, for example, gifted new textile artists appeared. In the British Isles, new life and innovation infused an old tradition. There were no patchwork shops; there were no guilds for mutual inspiration; American and English books on quilts and quilting were scarce. There was not much choice in fine cotton material, in calicoes or solids, nor in quilting threads and needles.

In some countries, including my home, Holland, collectors and museum textile curators became aware that old quilt treasures had been made during past centuries by great numbers of mostly anonymous needle-workers. These quilts were pulled out of drawers and attics and eventually received the recognition they deserved.

The newborn quiltmakers in Europe had to make do with what could be found in fabric stores and markets. This chapter is dedicated to some of these quilters-of-the-first-hour outside the United States, whom I asked to tell about their first experiences in quiltmaking. Very often silk fabrics played an important role in their creative start, either as main material or as accents or special effects, together with other textiles. A red silk thread through all their stories is that once they fell in love with silk, they were addicted for good. The first try only inspired them to go further and to explore as I have the wonderful possibilities and the mysterious character of this unique fabric.

AUSTRALIA

Thel Merry

There are many talented Australian quiltmakers who are inspired by the vast, diverse landscape and the rich, colorful flora and fauna of their country. Here, fiber artist Thel Merry depicts two frogs playing in a tangle of wisteria branches. *Tweedle-Dum and Tweedle-Dee* is made of Thel's own hand-batiked silk and is machine quilted.

Cynthia Morgan

Landscape or Illusion? II, made in 1997, portrays the central Australian landscape as seen from the air. Cynthia says, "This aerial view surprised me as it softened and diffused the ruggedness and harshness of the Outback terrain." She used hand-dyed silk fabrics for the background, backing, and binding. Silk organza overlay was dyed to add depth and diffuse the background. Several heavy silks were manipulated by random gathering, and then dyed. Thick silk yarn was hand-dyed and hand-sewn to the dyed background before overlaying the silk organza. Textured silks were positioned on top and attached by hand and machine. The quilt top was machine quilted from the bottom upward, using a variegated thread that enhances the colors in the quilt.

Tweedle-Dum and Tweedle-Dee
Thel Merry, Buderim, Australia. 30″ × 48″ (76cm × 122cm). *Tweedle-Dum and Tweedle-Dee* is a silk quilt for wall hanging use. It has been extensively machine quilted. The silk is Chinese twill, the padding is Dacron, and the dyes are naphtol. Both dipping and sponging on of dyes has been used. The batik waxing method has been used to draw the form as well as giving a textured effect to the foliage and background.

Cynthia employs the characteristic of silk that it does not burn with a flame. She manipulates and curls the edges of small silk pieces by burning them. Nice flower shapes can be obtained with this technique. Cynthia uses a soldering iron and she warns against using a flame, which may cause accidents.

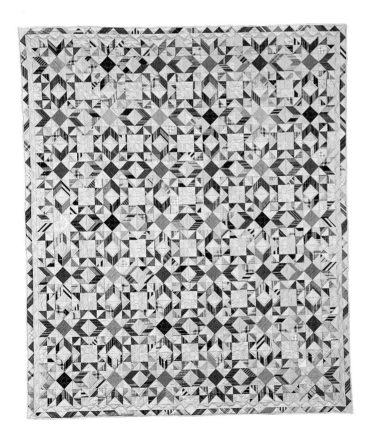

BELGIUM

Tineke van Hasselt

Intrigued by the *Wyoming Woman* block, Tineke van Hasselt redesigned it to make a quilt of small pieces of silk swatches. She received these scraps from a friend who had built a dollhouse for a grandchild, in which all the textiles, including curtains, bed coverlets, and wall tapestries, came from a silk sample book. She bought seven yards (about seven meters) of champagne-colored Indian doupion silk to combine with the scraps to create *Poppenkast*.

Poppenkast (dollhouse)
Tineke van Hasselt, Kapellen, Belgium, 1995. 91″ × 105″ (231cm × 267cm). Hand pieced, hand quilted; Indian doupion with silk samples. Photograph by Sam Dunlop.

CANADA

Ellen Adams

Ellen Adams made a series of six large quilts based on designs of elevator doors from buildings constructed during the 1920s and 1930s, in the style known as Art Deco. One of the six, *Squibb*, is an all-silk quilt. She says that "the curious, sometimes unrecognizable little creatures on the elevator doors seemed to require a more delicate interpretation than hard-edged appliqué. I used a liquid resist to divide the white Jacquard silk quilt top into long channels and brushed on different mixtures of blue-green dye. When it was dry, I quickly sketched the figures with a nearly dry dye brush so the darker colors could not spread very far. I cord-quilted the linework from the back and also stuffed the enclosed areas so they would be slightly raised from the surface." The zigzag stripes were appliquéd and the whole assembly was quilted through three layers along both sides of the stripes. This quilt took about three hundred hours to make.

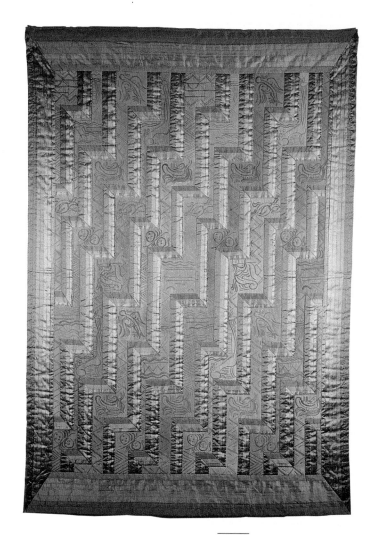

Jocelyne Patenaude

When her children were young, Jocelyne Patenaude started quiltmaking, using any material available. She grew into enjoying working with silks, and now she makes wall quilts of silks and bed quilts of wool. She created *Sage Femme* to suggest the midwife or wise woman who mediates transitions. Passages from dark to light to dark are conveyed through a blurring of edges. Jocelyne used recycled one hundred percent silk ties, which are made from all kinds of silk, thereby experimenting with a variety of textures. The hexagons are hand pieced with the English paper piecing method. She enjoyed continuing the traditional convention of using scraps and used clothing in the construction of this quilt, which is intended to be hung on the wall.

Valerie Hearder

Valerie Hearder was born in South Africa. She is an
autodidact who gathered her quilting knowledge
from books. Her first quilts were inspired by the
English medallion quilts that she made using the
English paper template method with some recycled
silks. Later, in Canada, she started making land-
scapes, and gradually silks took over from other
materials. Valerie made *Journey II* in 1996 for the
Quilt Expo Europa V in Lyon, France; it is one
hundred percent silk, predominantly taffetas, Thai
iridescent silks, and shantung. "I like to express
ideas of transcendence, and silk, to me, is a special
fabric with an almost spiritual quality to it . . . such
a connotation of richness and depth of color. . . ."

Journey II
Valerie Hearder, St. John's, Newfoundland,
Canada, 1996. 24″ × 38″ (61cm × 96cm).
Machine pieced, hand appliqué, machine
quilted. From the collection of Dr. John
and Francie Worthington. Photograph by
V. Hearder.

DENMARK

Charlotte Yde

Surprisingly, there is no quilt or patchwork tradition in Denmark—surprisingly, because so much excellent handwork is produced by Danish needle artists and because in neighboring Sweden so many quilts were made. The quilt revival reached Denmark in the 1980s and soon inspired one of the pioneers in Danish quiltmaking, Charlotte Yde. An art student at Copenhagen University, she received a degree at Håndarbejdets Fremme, the institution where the arts and techniques of needlework are taught. When she was bitten by the patchwork bug, Charlotte left traditional quiltmaking quickly and developed a personal, individual style in art quiltmaking.

In much of her work she combines cotton and silk. In *Valentine* and *Jars*, silks constitute more than half of the fabrics. She is not fond of using fusible interfacing to stabilize the silks, but prefers to treat the silks with light hands to prevent fraying because she believes that fusing influences the surface of the silk. When cutting silk strips, she likes to cut parallel to the selvage so fraying can be controlled.

Valentine* and *Jars
Charlotte Yde, Copenhagen, Denmark, 1995. Each 24″ × 24″ (60cm × 60cm). Machine pieced, machine quilted; half silks, half cottons.

Her Majesty, Queen Margrethe II of Denmark

Queen Margrethe II pursues the rich Danish tradition of fine needlework. For the services in Our Lady's Church, the Cathedral of Haderslev, a town in the southern part of Jutland, she designed and arranged four sets of furnishings in liturgical colors. Each set consists of a chasuble and an altar tapestry. The gold and white in one set symbolizes the feast of Easter Sunday and Advent Sunday. The materials are mostly silks from many countries that Her Royal Highness collected over a long period of time; the techniques are patchwork and machine appliqué.

Chasuble and alter tapestry
Designed and arranged by Her Majesty, Queen Margrethe II of Denmark for Our Lady's Church, Haderslev Cathedral, Denmark. Photograph by Jørgen Grønlund/Grønlund's Forlag.

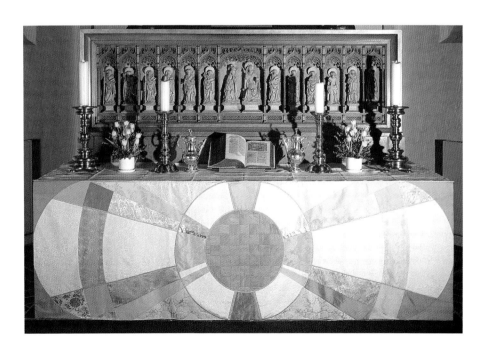

FRANCE

Soizik Labbens

Soizik Labbens fell in love with antique brocades from India, found in a market in Paris, and she made her first four silk quilts in 1984. When traveling, she looks for silks everywhere, and often friends and students give her small pieces. In her wall hanging *Pierres Précieuses*, the hand-dyed silks of the precious stones glitter and flash at the viewer.

Pierres Précieuses
Soizik Labbens, Nantes, France. 55″ × 39½″ (140cm × 100cm). Machine pieced, machine quilted; silks. Photograph by Soizik Labbens.

Renée Gosse

There is a long and beautiful heritage of richly stuffed and corded quilts in the southern French region, Provence. The Boutis Provençaux, also called Broderies de Marseille, have been produced for many centuries as textile art, mainly by professional needle-workers. These artists produced camisoles, petticoats, and crib and bed quilts with intricate patterns of flowers, vines, leaves, and other images. With tiny running stitches, tunnels were sewn to form the motifs, which were stuffed and corded, creating attractive raised designs. Although it is an extremely time-consuming technique, French women still produce boutis. Renée Gosse made *Jardin d'Orient* in 1996.

Jardin d'Orient, **Boutis Provençal**
Renée Gosse, Chatou, France, 1996. 49½″ × 51″ (126cm × 130cm). Hand stitched and hand stuffed, reversible; Soie Lyonnaise de Bianchini-Férier. Photograph by Alex Lévy.

It is a reversible quilt with no batting between the two layers of fabric, one of which is a Lyon silk, the other cotton.

Ildiko Français

Born in Hungary, Ildiko and her family fled to Canada when the Communists took over. After marrying a French diplomat, she led a nomadic life in countries all over the world. She bought silks and other textiles for dressmaking in many exotic places and possessed a substantial collection of scraps with no specific destination. When she visited her daughter in Canada, who had started making patchwork quilts, Ildiko knew immediately what all her scraps were waiting for. She employs many different styles and she uses various techniques. She amplifies her scraps with silks, which she dyes in the microwave.

In 1996, *Quilter's Newsletter Magazine* sponsored a contest, "Quilts, Artistic Expressions," in connection with Quilt Expo Europa V in Lyon. Ildiko was inspired by her favorite painter, Max Ernst, to make *Surrender of the Night*. Photographs were transferred to fabric and she painted trees, birds, and strange creatures on silk. She layered painted organza to achieve a transparent effect in the surrealistic landscape.

Surrender of the Night (**La Reddition de la Nuit**), **a Tribute to Max Ernst**
Ildiko Français, Vence, France, 1996. 68¾" × 52½" (173cm × 133cm). Machine pieced and machine quilted; various silks hand dyed by artist; also, artist's photographs transferred to fabric. Photograph by Ildiko Français.

Germany

Irene Kahmann

Irene Kahmann made her first silk quilt in 1985. Concerning her initial silk experience, she says: "Because silk fabric was expensive to buy and I needed a large variety, I started to dye and paint raw silk myself. I wash all the silk and obtain excellent results with it. But wash with care, like wool, and add vinegar in the end." She still loves to dye and paint silk fabrics because this guarantees exactly the color combinations she wants. Irene is another quilt artist who prefers to work with silks that don't fray too much in order to avoid using the fusible lining. She succeeds by working very carefully. *Thousands of Rain Drops* was made in memory of a trip to New Zealand, where she was overwhelmed by the Fjordland with glaciers, waterfalls, rain forests, and lakes. Irene loves to hand quilt. This quilt features Irene's superb hand appliqué and hand quilting.

Erika Odemer

"In 1984 I made my first quilt and it was a silk quilt, although then I did not know how to make a quilt like that. But today it still looks beautiful." Erika Odemer is a silk fabric collector. She is also one of those quiltmakers who knows which colors she wants, and she obtains them by dyeing and over-dyeing the silk fabrics herself, as for her quilt *Zwillinge*, or "Twins."

Dorle Stern-Straeter

Dorle Stern-Straeter's first patchwork quilt exposure was in the United States, where she lived for a number of years. She started using only cottons, but "after 1981 I mixed cotton with silk in my quilts. I did not especially buy silks, but there were always silk leftovers from dressmaking." She travels extensively and always finds fabrics, often silks. She is a fanatic dyer and painter, and creates the most wonderful pieces of personal graffiti silk. She dye-sprays silk background fabrics and enhances them with written graffiti. Pieces of these exclusive silks are used in *Graffiti VII*.

Thousands of Rain Drops
Irene Kahmann, Gröbenzell, Germany, 1991. 49″ × 70″ (125cm × 175cm). Machine pieced, hand appliquéd, hand quilted; various hand-dyed silks. Photograph by Irene Kahmann.

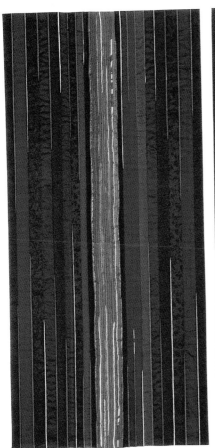
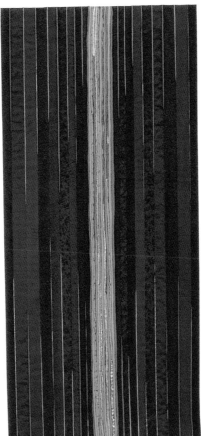

***Zwillinge* (Twins)**
Erika Odemer, Munich,
Germany, 1995. Each quilt
36" × 78" (92cm × 198cm).
Machine pieced, hand quilted;
mostly silks, some hand dyed
and over-dyed. Photograph by
Patricia Fliegauf.

***Graffiti* VII**
Dorle Stern-Straeter, Munich,
Germany, 1996. Each quilt 35½" ×
60½" (90cm × 154cm). Machine
pieced, hand quilted; hand painted
and hand written silks. Photograph
by Patricia Fliegauf.

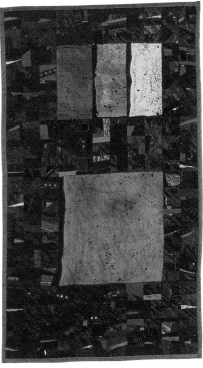

GREAT BRITAIN

Sally-Ann Boyd

Sally-Ann Boyd discovered the joy of using silk to make Seminole patchwork in an early stage of her quiltmaking. She loves to use a wide variety of silks with different weights and weaves: "Very few of them present a problem. Habutai is the worst for slipping and shot dupion the only one that frays badly. The trick is to handle no more than necessary and to avoid short cuts, i.e., pin and tack everything." She dyes most of her silks herself. "I cut the fabric into 20cm (8″) lengths (selvage to selvage), zigzag the two cut edges, wash in the washing machine, and dye. As my dye bath (it was a preserving pan, but I don't make jam anymore) holds approximately 200 grams, that means six to eight different silks go into the same dye bath." She uses a personally developed technique in her art quilts. She stitches the lining to the inter-lining, or the top layer to the inter-lining, as in her quilt *Emmeshes* V.

Emmeshes V
Sally-Ann Boyd, Cheltenham, England, 1996. 39″ × 39″ (99cm × 99cm). Machine pieced, hand quilted; hand and commercially dyed silks. Photograph by Richard Hookway.

Rita Humphry

Rita Humphry has always worked with silk. She loves the feel of it and the way it responds to light. She is well known for her embroidered, curved log cabin work in which "silk is the ideal fabric, as each strip is set at a slightly different angle to the one beside it, and the play of light intensifies the feeling of movement and life." Since Rita works on a paper foundation, she does not need stabilizer. She copes with the fraying by handling the strips as little as possible. *La Folia Variation I* shows a recent quilt in which Rita changed

La Folia Variation I
Rita Humphry, Tewkesbury, England, 1996. 44½″ × 29″ (113cm × 74cm). Hand pieced, hand quilted and embroidered; silks. Photograph by John Gibbons.

her style completely: the machine-pieced log cabins have been superceded by the exploration of all kinds of quilting, with surface stitchery and lace-work by hand in whites and pale colors.

Linda Straw

The exciting fantasy, unbridled imagination, and huge knowledge of fables and historic peculiarities are characteristics of Linda's work. There is so much to look at and every detail tells a whole story, so when one realizes that her tales are done in fabrics and mainly in silks, I think everybody must wonder how she did it. Shown here is a triptych, *Liberté Manger Gâteaux* (Freedom to Eat Cake), in which Linda narrates a story from Versailles just before the French Revolution in 1789. Linda's story: "The cook is saying, 'Here is your cake, Madam, but after the revolution I intend to open a restaurant in Paris.' Marie Antoinette, wearing a dress embroidered with symbols of the decadent *Ancien Regime*, has a flock of sheep in her hair. Louis XIV gazes from a portrait on the wall. The left panel shows well-known leaders of the revolution and peasant women demonstrating, with the Bastille and the guillotine in the distance. On the righthand panel we see the death of Marat (in the bathtub) in front of which stands a cartoon of the third estate being ridden by the church and the aristocracy. In the background rides the young Napoleon." The background is a fabric of wool and silk mix, and all the appliqué is silk. The embroidery thread is rayon 40. All work is done by machine.

Liberté Manger Gâteaux
(Freedom to Eat Cake)
Linda Straw, Leicestershire, England, 1996. 69″ × 39½″ (175cm × 100cm). Machine appliqué; wool/silk mix background, silk appliqué. Photograph by Nicholas Straw.

India

Wild silks were indigenous to India when cultivated silk arrived from China. The dowries of many brides included silk patchwork coverlets and embroidered and quilted silk coverlets. Not many have survived because in India it is traditional to use textile objects until they perish. A patchwork coverlet of exuberant silks made by an anonymous person has the charm of a piece made by someone who is not bound by rules. In my imagination I see a man or a woman quiltmaker, inspired by the deep, vibrant colors that are so characteristic of silks in the Far East, creating this uninhibited piece of patchwork. It was found in a small shop in Jodphur by quiltmaker Anne Scott, editor of *New Zealand Quilter* magazine.

Antique Rajasthani silk quilt
Unknown quilter, Jodphur, India. Collection of Anne Scott, Wellington, New Zealand. Photograph by Julia Brooke-White.

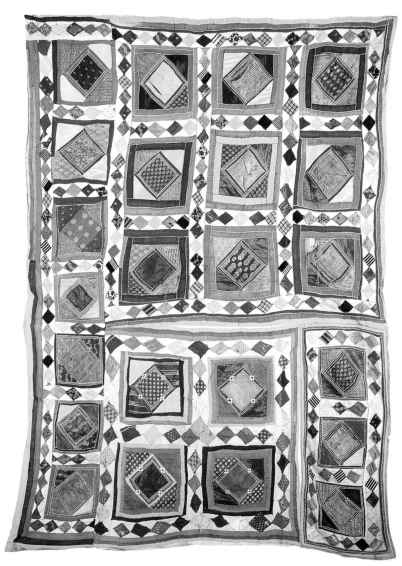

IRELAND

Ann Fahy

Ovals I

Ann Fahy, Galway, Ireland, 1996. 48″ × 48″ (122cm × 122cm). All hand-dyed silks, with cut out holes. Photograph by Ann Fahy.

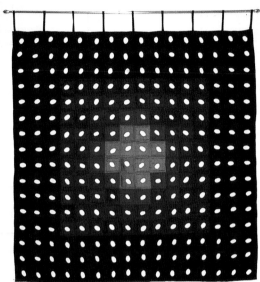

When she finds it necessary to stabilize a piece of silk, Ann Fahy prefers to use a fusible cotton. But she also uses a seam-overlocking stitch to prevent fraying. One of her latest quilts, *Ovals I*, is full of oval holes resembling white silk cocoons. This quilt is made in units of 3″ × 3″ (7.5cm × 7.5cm) each, with shades of blue on one side and a spectrum of colors on the other. Each unit is in three layers: two silk layers and the batting. The holes were stitched and then cut, and the layers turned to produce a hole with a rim of colors. These units were then stitched together with the seams on the multicolored side. This quilt won the Craft Council of Ireland award in 1996 and is now in the council's collection.

Ann Fleeton

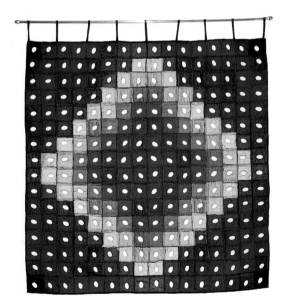

Ann made her first silk quilt in 1987. She describes this initial try: "I concentrated on overcoming the problem of frayed edges of small silk pieces and keeping the machine appliqué flat, while using a very limited sewing machine. Also, persistent electrical power cuts made work difficult as I struggled to finish the piece in time for an exhibition." For thin silks like habutai, she uses an ultralight fusible vilene or fusible cotton. She finds that the cotton is better but more costly, sometimes "the fusible is more expensive than the habutai!"

She dyes her silks in hot water acid dyes in powder form. "I use a stainless steel saucepan and put vinegar in the boiling water to transport the dye into the fabric. I rinse the fabric in clear water, and iron it when still damp. Mottled effects are achieved by folding, tying, or knotting the fabric before dyeing. The fabric can be immersed in the dye bath several times, using different colors. The whole operation is fairly quick; the drawback is that the vinegar makes the kitchen smell like a fish take-away!"

Ann manipulates her fabrics, embroidering and smocking them by machine before she cuts them. *Pond* is a quilt with intriguing surface textures.

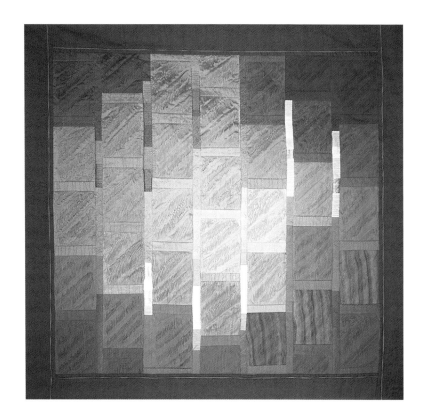

Pond
Ann Fleeton, Dublin, Ireland,
1996. 75″ × 72″
(191cm × 183cm). Hand
smocked, machine pieced,
machine embroidered, hand
quilted; dyed and painted
habutai and Indian doupion
silks. Photograph by Ann
Fleeton.

Phoenix I
Kakuko Okamura, Glenageary,
Ireland. 86″ × 79″
(220cm × 200cm).
Machine pieced, hand quilted;
mainly silk. Photograph by
Kakuko Okamura.

Kakuko Okamura

Kakuko Okamura was born in
China, grew up in Japan, and has
been living for many years in
Ireland, where she started quiltmaking in 1978. When her
mother sent her remnants of old
Japanese silk kimonos, of course
they were integrated into her
quiltmaking. She is a self-taught
quiltmaker, but has always been
interested in visual art, especially
painting and drawing. She enjoys
using fabrics as paints to make a
fabric picture. *Phoenix 1* is a study
in textured reds. Only for very
fine and thin silks does she use a
fusible, and occasionally she dyes
her silks.

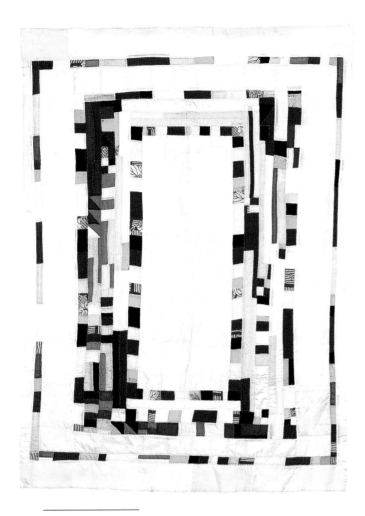

JAPAN

Junko Maeda

Junko Maeda made *Yohaku*, which means "blank space," from the linings of kimonos and kimono coats worn by her grandparents, parents, sisters, and herself. Through her quilts she hopes to convey the message of the good life in Japan, especially that of bygone days.

Michiko Shima

Michiko started making small things with fabric when she was nine years old, which led to taking a patchwork class in 1979. *Rakuren* is made from old Japanese silks. This quilt is one of the striking examples of an American traditional design that has been personalized in an unmistakably Japanese manner.

Yohaku (blank space)
Junko Maeda, Kanagawa, Japan, 1994. 47½″ × 63″ (120cm × 160cm). Hand pieced, hand quilted; silk kimono linings. Photograph by Yutaka Takayama.

Rakuren
Michiko Shima, Gifu, Japan, 1996. 73½″ × 79″ (186cm × 200cm). Old Japanese silk.

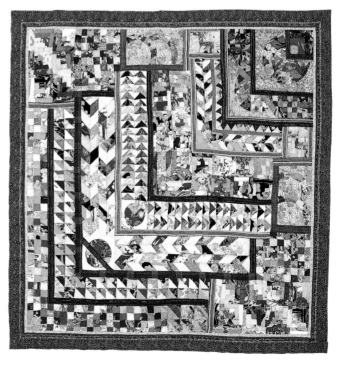

Atsuko Ohta

Atsuko works with the famous magazine *Patchwork Quilt Tsushin* in Tokyo. She fell in love with the colors and embroidery on an old, torn-apart kimono which she bought as pieces of fabric. The beauty of the antique fabric was preserved by Atsuko in the design of *Kimono Fantasy*.

THE NETHERLANDS

Ans Schipper-Vermeiren

A fairly new and inexperienced quilter at the time, Ans Schipper-Vermeiren composed a quilt of little silk squares in many colors and textures. Inspired by the colors of the tulip fields when Ans flew over western Holland, this quilt reveals her refined sense of color. Ans lives on a farm, where she attends her flock of Hampshiredown sheep. She has much more time to design and construct new quilts since leaving a part-time job.

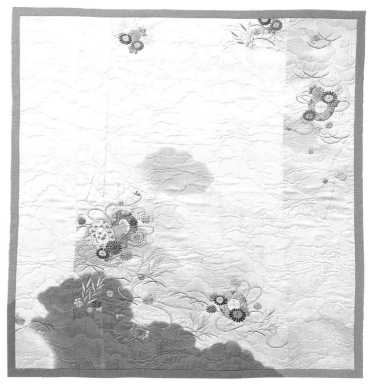

Kimono Fantasy
Atsuko Ohta, Tokyo, Japan, 1992. 63″ × 65″ (160cm × 165cm). Hand pieced and hand quilted with silk thread; old kimono fabric.

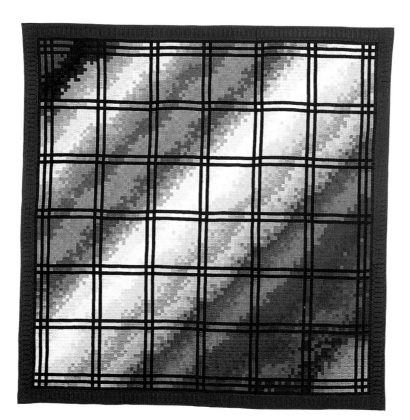

Bulb Fields
Ans Schipper-Vermeiren, Hagestein, the Netherlands, 1994. 112″ × 112″ (290cm × 290cm). Hand and machine pieced, hand quilted. Photograph by Sam Dunlop.

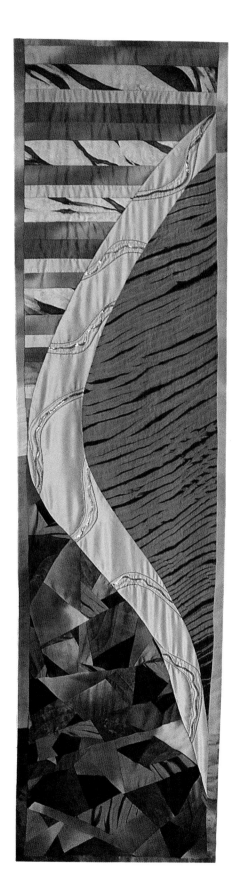

Hans Sterkenburg

Hans Sterkenburg wanted to make a silk quilt for one of her sons. She chose a very simple shape, triangles, for all the busy plaids and striped silks she had collected, and united them with light triangles in various white silks.

Lijnenspel (**Lines at Play**)
Hans Sterkenburg, Gorinchem, the Netherlands, 1997.
68¼″ × 68¼″
(173cm × 173cm). Machine pieced, hand quilted; Indian doupion, Thai silk, and ikat. Photograph by Sam Dunlop.

Nelleke van de Wege-van Sevenhoven

Nelleke is a full-time schoolteacher. Years ago her hobby was silk painting, and she started quiltmaking in order to extend the use of all her colorful silks. On nice summer days during her vacations, you may find her in the yard of her farm in northern Holland, busily dyeing lengths of silk fabric in many colors. These silks will find their way into the art quilts she creates in her free time during long winter evenings.

Freedom
Nelleke van de Wege-van Sevenhoven, Lucaswolde, the Netherlands, 1997. 35½″ × 57½″
(90cm × 146cm). Machine pieced, hand quilted; ikat silk, arashi-shibori, hand-painted crepe, habutai, noil, shantung, and doupion silks, metal and silk threads.

In *Freedom*, she included crepe de chine, crepe satin, hunan, doupions, and bourettes; her dyeing techniques include different kinds of shibori, silkscreen printing, and airbrushing. As embellishment she used metal thread embroidery, done by machine, and she hand quilted with silk and metal threads.

Joop Smits

When Joop Smits visited the Baltimore Quilt exposition in the Metropolitan Museum in New York in 1981, she was very impressed by the beauty of the quilts. She planned to create a Baltimore quilt herself one day, and started collecting suitable cotton fabrics. Next, she designed her own patterns. The resulting quilt is a gorgeous piece of needleart work, but because she used very few pieces of silk, it does not qualify for this book. I asked Joop if she would consider making a small Baltimore wall hanging in all-silk fabrics. She created *Spring in Bilthoven*, in which she used new silks as well as silks from her deceased mother's dresses. Only very thin silks are stabilized with a fusible. The three-dimensional flowers are rouched organza and chiffon silk fabrics, without a fusible. Joop used filament silk thread, which was a discovery for her; she will only use filament thread in future appliqué quilts. She advises against using silks in a first try at appliqué.

Spring in Bilthoven
Joop Smits, Bilthoven, the Netherlands, 1997. 24″ × 24″ (61cm × 61cm). Hand appliquéd, hand quilted; silk scraps on habutai (pongee silk). Photograph by Sharon Risedorph.

Nicky van den Berg

Nicky has a full-time job, but manages to find time to make quilts. She has pieced and hand quilted many traditional block and medallion quilts, and wanted to try something she had not done before. Inspired by a Quaker crazy quilt she saw in a book, she decided to incorporate her wedding dress, a wild tussah silk minicreation from the 1960s, into a crazy quilt. The result is *Marriage in Pieces*, in which she combined the tussah with Indian

Marriage in Pieces
Nicky van den Berg, Giessen-
burg, the Netherlands, 1997. 85″
× 96½″ (215cm × 245cm).
Machine pieced, hand quilted;
tussah, bourette, and other silks.
Photograph by Sharon
Risedorph.

doupion, bourette, and exclusive Thai plaid
sarong silks.

Anne de Vries Robbé

Anne wanted to use the silks from the
evening dresses of a long-ago life of enter-
taining. Pieces of every blouse and gown
she wore as hostess were put into the quilt,
in a variation of the *Delectable Mountains*
pattern. She bought only the light silks used
for the background spaces. Anne says she
derived great satisfaction from making this
quilt, which she calls *Pieces of My Past*.

Pieces of My Past
Anne de Vries Robbé, Dalem,
the Netherlands, 1997. 91″ × 91″
(230cm × 230cm). Machine
pieced, hand quilted; Indian
doupion and various other silks.
Photograph by Sharon
Risedorph.

New Zealand

Ruth Cumming

Initially, says Ruth, "I was inspired by a Tumbling Blocks quilt made by Mrs. James Newman in 1880. As I stitched I found that the lovely silks often reminded me of illustrations for fairy tales. So, for the border I designed trailing thorns to shield the jewels of the sleeping princess." Ruth used black silk velvet in *Luxurious Illusions*, and Thai silks in many colors for the hexagons appliquéd onto the black velvet. Instead of batting, she placed a layer of cotton lawn on the back of the velvet to stabilize it while appliquéing. Ruth says that she will never appliqué on velvet again because it moves so much, but she also admires the wonderful glow it gives to the finished piece.

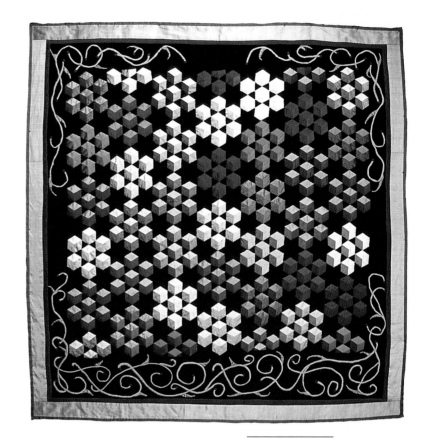

Luxurious Illusions
Ruth Cumming, Waikanae, Wellington, New Zealand, 1996. 61½″ × 64″ (156cm × 162cm). Silk hexagons hand appliquéd to silk velvet.

Jill Bezencon

Giza was Jill Bezencon's answer to the Tribute to Triangles Challenge of the National Association of New Zealand Quilters. A friend dyed the apricot silk background with "blobs" of green, blue, red, and yellow for the appliqué. She stabilized the entire two meters with Vlisofix, a paper-backed webbing, which enabled her to cut the large 60° background triangle and draw the other triangles from the "blobs." The main triangle was ironed onto English batting, on which she planned the placement of the smaller triangles. For embellishment, Jill chose paua shell buttons, lace, cord, beads, and junk shop plastic buttons.

Giza
Jill Bezencon, Army Bay, Hibiscus Coast, New Zealand. Machine appliqué; hand-dyed silks by Janet Ryan. Owned by Ann Jolly, Hamilton, New Zealand. Photograph by Janet Ryan, Devonport, Auckland, New Zealand.

Norway

Solfrid Meek Al-Kasim

"Growing up in Norway during and after World War II, silk was just a fairy-tale word that encompassed everything we then lacked. A word that in my dreams took me to exotic, faraway places." Her aunt's wedding dress was made of parachute silk; a little girl then, Solfrid Meek Al-Kasim touched real silk for the first time, a sensation and excitement she never forgot. Later, when she came to live for a number of years in Iraq with her husband, she was exposed to many kinds of silks in the bazaars. Her flight attendant sisters also brought her silks from the Far East, so no wonder she chose silk for her textile art.

Oss Selv Nok is a self-critical portrait of the neo-chauvinism that swept Norway in 1994. Triggered by the successful Winter Olympic Games at Lillehammer, it culminated in November, when in a national referendum a majority of the population voted not to join the European Union. Nationalism is portrayed as the Madonna dressed in a national costume. The same year also saw a virtual closure of Norway's borders to political refugees—hence the "no entry" signs in the top corners. The figure of the dancing couple is an old Norwegian knitting pattern portraying the ritual of self-righteousness. The Viking ships on the borders are there to further emphasize the historical heritage of Norway as a nation. This quilt is Solfrid's way of disagreeing with Norway's political attitude.

Saudi Arabia

Marjo Aarts

Marjo Aarts bought two meters of black and gold Jinny Beyer/RJR border print and some black and gold Indian doupion silks. She intended to make lots of pillows, all the same size and pattern, varying only the template placement on the border print and the placement of the black and gold silks. When she had finished several blocks, she was intrigued by the composition they formed together, and she decided to make a whole quilt. Says Marjo, "Like the light that shines through the old church windows onto the mosaic floor, this quilt has been made to please the eyes with that same ray of sunlight."

SOUTH AFRICA

Ginny Koumantarakis

Ginny Koumantarakis has a gift for mathematics. Her quilt *It's All About Numbers* was inspired by two things: the Vedic multiplication square, which was brought to the West by Leonardo Fibonacci of Pisa (1170–1240) via the Arabs of North Africa. Secondly, she was moved by the glorious colors and textures of the small swatches of silks and satins given to her by her interior decorator sister. These were the ideal fabrics to realize her inspiration. Ginny says that this quilt "is a tribute to all the hidden patterns in nature and to those moments of awareness in our lives when we recognize them."

Old Roman Floor
Marjo Aarts, Riyadh, Saudi Arabia, 1996. 63" × 63" (160cm × 160cm). Hand pieced, hand quilted. Photograph by Sam Dunlop.

It's All About Numbers
Ginny Koumantarakis, Westville, Kwazulu Natal, South Africa, 1995. 30" × 30" (76cm × 76cm). Hand pieced, hand quilted; silk samples.

Judy Breytenbach

Judy loves working with silk fabrics because of their rich, vibrant colors. *African Mosaic* is constructed from a combination of silks and ethnic cottons, with the added texture of mohair and wool fringing. The elongated, narrow shape of the quilt reflects Judy's African design inspiration.

UNITED STATES OF AMERICA

Yvonne Porcella

Yvonne Porcella is one of the best-known textile artists of the United States. One of her many activities is creating pieced and appliquéd silk quilts for which she developed her own dyeing techniques. Her appliquéd flowers and grapes in *Garden Blossoms* are small pieces of silk, burned carefully around the edges in the lower part of a candle flame, a process described in her book *Colors Changing Hue*.

African Mosaic
Judy Breytenbach, Kloof, South Africa, 1996. 55″ × 21¾″ (140cm × 55cm). Silk with ethnic fabric. Photograph by Judy Breytenbach.

Garden Blossoms
Yvonne Porcella, Modesto, California, U.S.A., 1992. 44″ × 34″ (112cm × 86cm). Hand-painted silks, burned silk appliqué. Private collection. Photograph by Sharon Risedorph.

Susan C. Druding

Susan created a most unusual crazy quilt, *Silk Is Busting Out All Over.* A variety of wild tussah silks form the traditional blocks in the upper half of the quilt. Then, suddenly, a bunch of lively cocoons invade the lower part, adding a delightful surprise and visual interest.

N. Amanda Ford and Jeannette Kuvin Oren

Two quilt artists, living hundreds of miles apart, succeed beautifully in creating Judaic fiber art while collaborating long distance. For their Torah covers and Ark curtains they choose silks of many different kinds because of silk's "remarkable affinity for color and texture." In order to cope with the slippery silks, they employ freezer paper, which stabilizes each piece. The Ark curtain *Parting of the Waters* was created for Heska Amuna Synagogue in Knoxville, Tennessee. The curtain opens in the middle and the scene depicts the opening of the Red Sea, with the pillar of fire that protected the Israelites behind the opening waters. The curtain was quilted and embellished with silver to match the epoxy of the synagogue's huge stained-glass window.

Silk Is Busting Out All Over
Susan C. Druding, Berkeley, California, U.S.A., 1996. 18″ × 24″ (45.5cm × 61cm). Batting, cocoons, and threads are all entirely silk.

Ann Johnston

Ann is a versatile quilt artist who started silk quiltmaking about fifteen years ago when she was experimenting with fabric paints and dyes and wanted surface excitement. Her work is both contemporary and figurative; it includes hand and machine piecing and quilting, appliqué, and a whole range of dye and paint techniques.

Ann says, "When I saw how its [silk's] luminosity shows the relief of the quilting, I was hooked. I use mostly two weights of a firmly woven broadcloth, called fuji. I also use shantung and various habutai types, which give

me some textures. Since I dye all my fabric, I can buy bulk so that the cost is not prohibitive. Dyeing [silk] fabric requires thorough washing at high temperatures, and the silk seems very tough to me, not the fragile stuff I had always thought. [Author's comment: the dyes Ann uses require thorough washing, not all dyes do.] Silk seems to have a give in all directions when sewing with it, and it slips under the presser foot, so I use a walking foot with all my piecing. That give in all directions is an advantage when you piece curves, particularly with freehand cuts as in *Red River*. The silk seems to accept the curves and presses down well. My attitude is that silk is a magic fiber, tough and flexible, and worth every penny."

Parting of the Waters,
synagogue Ark curtain
N. Amanda Ford, Cabin John, Maryland, U.S.A., and Jeannette Kuvin Oren, Woodbridge, Connecticut, U.S.A., 1998. 56″ × 67″ (142cm × 170cm). Machine pieced, embellished with silver ribbons and cords; hand-dyed silks. Photograph by Breger and Associates.

Red River
Ann Johnston, Lake Oswego, Oregon, U.S.A., 1995. 12″ × 21″ (30.5cm × 53.5cm). Machine pieced and quilted; hand-dyed silks. Photograph by Bill Bachhuber.

WORKING WITH SILK

Dutch Touch
Hanne Vibeke de Koning-Stapel, 1992. 94″ × 94″ (240cm × 240cm). Machine pieced, hand quilted; blue and red Dutch chintz and white Indian doupion silk. Photograph by Sam Dunlop.

It is clear from the previous chapters that silks have been widely used in quiltmaking from early days, and that the tradition of sewing with silk fabrics is carried forth by a great number of quilters around the world. In this chapter, by dispelling some prejudices about the characteristics of silk, my goal is to reach hesitant quilters—and to give you confidence that silk will work for you also. I hope that you will enjoy your first silk experience, a way to bring a new level of innovation into your quiltmaking.

WHO'S AFRAID OF SILK? DISPELLING SOME MYTHS

I have often wondered why so few quiltmakers choose to work with silk fabrics. From talking with quilters, I have come to the conclusion that there are several misconceptions about silk, built on wrong assumptions.

Among the reasons why quiltmakers avoid silk fabrics, these three may be the most common: silk is expensive and hard to find, silk is fragile and delicate, and silk is difficult to work with because it is slippery and ravels easily.

Myth 1: Silk Is Expensive and Hard to Find

Within the huge range of silk fabrics there are much greater differences in qualities, weaves, and weights than in cotton fabrics. So there is also a huge variation in prices, from reasonable to extremely expensive. Simple silks, like Indian doupion, Chinese habutai and shantung, and Thai silk, the types most apt to be used in quiltmaking, are reasonably priced, and in many countries they are readily available in good fabric stores or from mail-order firms. Friends in many countries sent me addresses where they buy their silks, and I have also discovered numerous fabric shops that carry silk fabrics in their collections. Some of these shops provide catalog and mail-order services (see Resources to find one convenient for you).

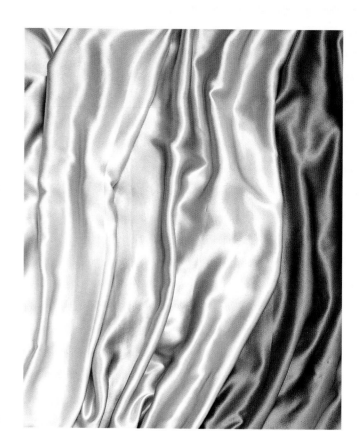

You may not want to make a large quilt using expensive brocades, but you might try to add little bits of silk, satin, damask, or Jacquard to a quilt to make it look rich and luxurious for just a little extra cost. If you want to work with silks at low cost, consider buying white silks, which are less expensive than the dyed ones. It is great fun to experiment with dyeing them yourself.

Myth 2: Silk Is Fragile and Delicate

Most silks are no more fragile than other textiles, provided the silk is treated well and protected from its enemies (some kinds *are* delicate: for instance, gossamer chiffons and organzas). The silk fiber itself yields an extremely strong and hard-wearing fabric, but what may make silk less strong is the effect of the hidden processes of dyeing and finishing. These processes are unavoidable in all textile manufacturing, and beyond control of the consumer. Proof of silk's durability lies in the fact that some of the oldest archaeological textile finds are silk, like the forty-seven-hundred-year-old piece of *Bombyx mori* silk in the bamboo basket found in China (see page 4), and in the many surviving silk quilts from the seventeenth and eighteenth centuries.

I think the image of fragility is based on the fact that silk fabrics of the Victorian period, from about 1850 to 1900, were heavily weighted with metal salts because fashion prescribed that women should wear rustling taffeta skirts. This rustling, also called scroop, was achieved by treating the silk fibers with deadly metals, which resulted in the deterioration of these maltreated fibers. The same metal salts, especially iron and tin salts, were used as mordants to fix dyes. You can read more about weighting, the damage it caused, and the economic aspects of this practice in Chapter 3.

Myth 3: It Is Difficult to Work with Silk

Before they try out silk, many quilters believe that it is tough to work with because it is slippery, it frays badly, and it splits easily in the seams. If you are afraid of silk because of these properties, there is a simple solution: stabilize silk fabrics by ironing the thinnest fusible interfacings to the back of the silk. In the United States and Europe there are several fusibles that are fine enough to qualify for light- and medium-weight silks. Although I dislike the idea of combining an artificial product containing an adhesive with silk, this has worked for me for more than fifteen years. Fusing enables me to work easily with the wonderful properties of silk, a process otherwise fraught with problems. Note, however, that not all silk quiltmakers use a fusible bonding; they employ other solutions. In Chapter 5, several quilt-makers reveal their personal methods.

TO FUSE OR NOT TO FUSE?

It was a "live and learn" experience in 1981 when I made my first silk quilt, *Drunkard's Path*, shown on pages 20–21. I had made several 11″ (28cm) blocks of this pattern from Indian doupion silks, with a regular ¼″ (0.5cm) seam allowance and a layer of thin, loosely woven muslin as a stabilizer. For

whatever baffling reason, I left the stack of blocks on a sofa, where somebody without a quilt education happened to sit down. Seams in several blocks split open. Even if this treatment was rougher than the usual wear and tear on a quilt, it was clear that I would have to solve this problem before going further, as I was not planning to give up on silk. Bonding with fusible interfacing was the solution. Whenever I meet a quiltmaker who objects that fusibles make the silk thick and stiff, I conclude that she uses the wrong interfacing and invite her to handle any of my silk quilts; none of them feel or look stiff.

Iron the fusible to the silk, carefully following the manufacturer's instructions. Be sure to eliminate all wrinkles first by steam pressing the entire piece of silk fabric, on the wrong side (if there is a difference between right and wrong sides); then place the fusible interfacing with the adhesive side down on the (wrong) side of the silk fabric. I start in the upper right corner and press each place five to six seconds (be sure to follow the manufacturer's advice), moving toward the left upper corner. The iron continuously overlaps itself. Beware of the fact that most fusible interfacings tolerate less heat from the iron than the silk fabrics.

I prefer to press a full length of fusible onto a full width of silk fabric. One yard of fusible will not cover a whole width of silk, usually 36″ to 37″ (92cm to 95cm) wide; therefore, I advise buying interfacing to accommodate the most common width of silk fabrics. When adopting this method, the crosswise stretch of a knitted, woven, or nonwoven fusible is put on the lengthwise warp threads that stretch less than the crosswise weft threads.

Some of the products may require use of a pressing cloth or steam. Read the instructions and test first on a small piece. Vlieseline has a printed text in the selvage that I always discard because the blue ink may show through or come off.

You may wonder about the durability of fusible interfacings. The German manufacturer of Vlieseline has assured me that the fusible material will be as durable as the silk fabrics and that it is safe for hand washing and chemical dry cleaning. The adhesive will not come loose.

Fusible Interfacings

The fusible interfacings I recommend are:

Softline Vlieseline/Vilene/Fliselina H 180®. Nonwoven, available in white and black. Suitable for both hand and machine piecing. Available in Europe, Australia, and New Zealand, and my absolute favorite.

Pellon® #906 Fusible Nonwoven Interfacing for Sheer to Lightweight Fabrics. Suitable for machine piecing; may be hard for hand piecing. Available in the United States.

Stacy #130 Easy-Knit® Fusible Knit Interfacing & Underlining. Comes in white and black. Suitable for both hand and machine piecing.

Touch o' Gold™. Woven rayon. Comes in white, ecru, and black. Best for machine piecing.

I like to keep a stock of my favorite fusible interfacings in light and dark colors, so that when I buy a piece of silk I can fuse it and use it immediately.

Cutting and Tearing Silk

In the stores where I buy silk fabrics, both cutting and tearing are used. Plain weaves such as habutai, China silk, Indian doupion, and even organza can be ripped, but there is always loss of several threads, which can be avoided by cutting with a scissors or rotary cutter. If you want to be sure that your cut is on the grain, in many silks the weft (crosswise) thread is strong enough to be pulled. In doupion silks, it's easy to follow one of the irregular weft threads when cutting. Plain weaves with heavily twisted yarns like crepe de chine, spun silks like bourettes (noils), and wild silks like tussahs should be cut. Twill and ribbed weaves also must be cut.

Most silk fabrics can only be torn in one direction, from selvage to selvage. The selvages are strong and must be cut. Tussah and Indian doupion will fray considerably more when torn or cut from selvage to selvage, than when cut parallel to the selvages. Others, such as bourette or crepe de chine, will hardly fray at all.

A large piece of silk fabric without a fusible may be slippery and unmanageable on the cutting mat. This problem is solved by putting a piece of cotton fabric or flannel under the silk fabric, leaving a narrow strip on the cutting mat free where you're going to cut. Fold the largest piece of fabric on the mat so that it does not hang heavily off the mat.

Quilting Supplies

Needles and Pins

Throw away needles and pins with blunt tips that may damage silks. Use only ultrafine pins. Silk pins are not necessarily the finest; some Japanese glass-headed pins and pleating pins are thinner.

For hand piecing and quilting, I prefer size #10 or #12 needles, which are thin enough for fine silk. When machine piecing, a size 10/12 needle (European size 75/80) is the right size for silks *lined with fusible interfacing*. Without interfacing, a size 9/10 (European 65/70) is the best. Before starting a silk project, testing the needle size on scraps is advisable. A fresh needle for every ten to twelve hours of machine sewing is essential!

Silk Threads

When working with silk fabrics, I prefer to use silk thread because of the compatible properties, elasticity, and flexibility. Because silk fiber is the strongest of all natural fibers, the construction thread need not be thick to be strong. The thickness of the thread should equal that of the weft (cross-wise) threads of the silk fabric, or the average of weft and warp threads, in case yarns of different weight are used.

Not all quiltmakers give much attention to the choice of construction thread. Moreover, many quiltmakers may not be aware that in silk construction thread, there is a choice between filament and spun silk thread.

Filament silk thread is mainly made in Japan. This thread is quite expensive, but it has a beautiful shine and comes in a huge range of wonderful colors. The smooth filament thread glides through the fabric layers, which makes it wonderful for hand piecing and quilting. It comes on spools of two-ply or three-ply: the two-ply is thinner, but strong enough for lightweight silks. Filament thread will not leave lint in your sewing machine. (See Resources for thread suppliers).

Spun silk thread is less expensive, but still more costly than cotton or polyester. I like to use the spun silk thread manufactured in Germany by Gütermann. It comes on spools of 110 yards (100 meters) and is ideal to work with on the sewing machine, as well as for hand piecing and quilting. Under a microscope, filament thread has a smooth surface, while spun thread, made of short fibers twined together, has a fluffy surface. Consequently, spun silk thread is a fraction less smooth and it will leave some lint in your sewing machine.

If you cannot find either kind of silk thread, the next best is cotton and rayon thread. I prefer to baste silk quilts with filament thread—the height of decadence—safeguarding against holes in the silk fabrics. Then I recycle the "basting thread" and use it for the next quilt.

At the end of the nineteenth century, a much broader variety of silk thread was offered by various factories in the United States and Europe than what is available today. The Corticelli Silk Mills in America imported raw silk from Asia and manufactured machine twist silk, sewing silk, twisted embroidery silk, buttonhole silk, lampshade silk, dental floss, surgeons' darning silk, and many more varieties.

For the consumer, it is not always easy to interpret the figures and codes on the spools of sewing thread. With each brand the manufacturer uses numbers for colors, and specifies the number of yards or meters on the spool. When a spool is marked 50 (silk) weight, this indicates a medium-sized thread; 100 (silk) weight indicates a thread with a finer diameter; the much thicker buttonhole thread is 8 weight.

Batting

The choice of batting is important; it should not be thick and fluffy. Several manufacturers discovered that there is a market for silk batting, and I tried several kinds, which I purchased from suppliers listed in Resources. However, silk batting is considerably more expensive than any other kind of batting. It is hardly softer to quilt through, and since this extravagant luxury is not really visible, you might choose to spend money on silks for the quilt top and use one of the excellent thin cotton battings that hand quilt smoothly.

MARKING SILKS

Any marking tools normally used with cotton can also be used with silk. I prefer a hard pencil for tracing quilting patterns on light silks. On damask or satin a softer pencil is preferable to avoid snagging the fabric. Draw the lines as lightly as possible; it is difficult, if not impossible, to erase too-heavy pencil marks. However, in my experience they do vanish when the quilt is dry-cleaned. A blue water-erasable pen can also be used; they don't seem to damage silk fabrics as long as the lines are removed by gently spraying the fabric with water, and not emersing it. On dark silks, I usually mark with white or pastel-colored chalk powder. As always, test these methods first!

Quilting Silks

Some quilters may suppose that an extra layer of fusible interfacing makes quilting harder. When I am hand quilting fused silk, I have no trouble taking the same small stitches as when hand quilting cottons. When the fusible is added to India or Thai silks, it's no thicker or harder to get through than quilters' cottons. Silk is very light. The specific weight of silk is 1.31, compared to that of cotton, 1.56.

While I was doing research to write this book and had no time to hand quilt, I asked Gayle Ropp of Virginia to quilt *Polyhymnia*, in which all the silks are lined with Vlieseline 180. Gayle wrote: "It's quilting beautifully and spoiling me when I go back to cotton." She used Hobb's dark Polydown batting and Gütermann silk thread. The backing is a mixed sixty percent silk/forty percent cotton, dyed deep purple in the washing machine at 140°F (60°C).

Some quiltmakers warn against using quilting hoops for silk. I quilt my silk quilts either in a large frame or in a hoop. I need strong tension in order to sew small stitches, and I never encountered any slashed-seam problems.

Detail of hand quilting on
Stella Florealis

Caring for Silks and Silk Quilts

The smooth silk fiber absorbs dye wonderfully, but this also means that the fiber readily absorbs dirt. Work with clean, dry hands and don't use hand lotion just prior to working on silk. Dust and dirt may cause silk to disintegrate at an earlier age than necessary.

Silk is well known for its insulating property: warm in the winter and cool in the summer. However, when used in garments, it should be taken into consideration that silk is damaged by human perspiration, and perhaps even more by antiperspirants. It is preferable to use silk for loose-fitting garments like kimonos. Besides perspiration, silk has a few additional enemies.

While the other animal fiber, wool, may be ruined by moths, they are not a threat to clean silk, because moth does not eat moth. However, dust and dirt in silk may attract moths, and silverfish, if hard pressed, may eat silk, while mice love to line their nests with silk if they get the chance.

Silk and sunlight do not go well together, because sun rays destroy the protein fiber. Quilt and fabric lovers are aware of the dangers and would not think of leaving textiles or quilts in the sun. I have been told that moon rays are even more devastating than those of the sun.

Washing Silks

Washing instructions for silk garments almost always recommend "dry clean only." This often is a protection for the manufacturer, to safeguard against claims of customers who carelessly wash a silk blouse in the washing machine together with T-shirts. In the case of a garment with intricate inside constructions and those made of wild tussah silks, it's wise to bring the piece to a dry cleaner who knows and cares about the treatment of silk.

You can wash most mulberry silk fabrics (and simple dresses of this material), and some will even gain in luster and drape. Most kinds of silk will shrink when washed. Use a mild soap or detergent especially developed for silk. Liquid Ivory, Orvus, and Castile soap are products sold in the United States; Tenestar is a German product for the European market. Baby shampoo (without conditioner) is perfect. It is most important that your soap or detergent contain no chlorine or optical brighteners.

Place the silk in lukewarm, almost cool, water in which liquid soap or detergent is dissolved; gently swish the material with your hands for at most sixty seconds. Rinse several times in cool water. In the final rinse, use cold water and add a small amount of white vinegar to set the dyes and neutralize possible soap residue. Press out the water carefully; do not wring silk. Let it drip-dry, hanging or laying flat, or dry in a terry towel. You can stretch silk fabric while wet, but it will regain its original size when dry.

Hand-painted silk by Ineke van Buuren, the Netherlands

Do not be surprised if your brightly colored silks bleed when you wash them. Excess dye is washed out, and probably this will not affect the brightness of the color. In iridescent silks, it may be only the warp or the weft thread that bleeds, and this bleeding may affect yarns of the other color. When I washed a bright magenta iridescent silk several times and it kept bleeding, which affected the green warp yarns, I decided to avoid factors that may soil my silk quilts, to vacuum them regularly and, in case of hazard, to take no risk and to have a patchwork quilt dry cleaned.

Never bleach silk with chlorine or enzyme bleaches, which will damage the silk irreparably. If you absolutely must bleach silk, use liquid hydrogen peroxide and be sure to experiment on a small piece first. Still, this procedure may weaken the fabric.

Ironing Silks

Iron or press silk fabrics while still damp. They will dry quickly, and if you missed the chance to iron the silk while damp, this will not matter. Most kinds of silk can be ironed with steam on the wrong side without a pressing cloth. You may want to test a small piece first. If you work with moiré, though, extra attention is necessary because this fabric has been treated in a special way to obtain the wavy, watered appearance, and it may react adversely to watery steam. Waterspots are difficult to remove, so if your steam iron leaks or "spits" you will definitely need a pressing cloth. A water stain on a piece of silk is usually cured by dipping the whole piece in water and ironing it when half dry. Do not use spray starch, which may stain your silk fabric.

Mulberry silk can be ironed at a temperature of 160°C (320°F), or between silk and wool settings, while the temperature for wild silk should be a little lower at 130°C (265°F). Spend a little extra time in testing the options. When I am piecing, I always press from the right side without a pressing cloth. I have become quite ruthless in this practice, and I have never experienced the silk becoming shiny. Note that the correct movement of the iron is up and down, not gliding.

Again, it is wise to test first. Ironing from the wrong side after the silk is lined with a fusible interfacing is very awkward.

Dry Cleaning Silks and Silk Quilts

Since silk quilts are "best quilts," made for show and not typically used as blankets, the question of cleaning must be addressed only once over many years. Several of my silk quilts have been dry cleaned by expert cleaners, and they regained their original luster without any negative effect.

Instead of washing or sending to the dry cleaner, you may want to treat your silk quilt to vacuum cleaning once every six months to a year. This is a treatment that textile curators recommend for antique quilts because dust and invisible dirt (pollution) will affect any textile negatively, and the protein fibers wool and silk are especially sensitive.

The method is simple: a piece of fiberglass screening is taped off on all four sides in order to eliminate sharp points. The screening is put on top of the quilt, laying flat on a firm and protected layer. With the mouth of the vacuum smooth and clean, and possibly protected with a nylon pantyhose, cautiously vacuum the whole surface of the quilt, front and back, with the power at its lowest setting.

Small pieces of antique kimono or sarong silks may be dry cleaned at home with solvents like Carbona and Energine (in the U.S.A.) and White Spirit (in Europe). Fill one-third of a 1- to 1.5-gallon (5-liter) glass jar with the solvent, put small pieces of silk in the jar, close the lid and shake it gently for half a minute. Then, squeezing softly in order to leave as much of the solvent as possible in the jar, pull your silk out of the jar clean and bright. Hang to dry on a hanger; in less than five minutes, it's dry and needs no ironing. **Warning:** Because the solvent is combustible (flammable), always practice this home dry cleaning outdoors and away from open fire.

Storing Silks and Silk Quilts

When storing pieces of silk fabric, sharp folds should be avoided because silk may eventually crack in sharp folds. It is better to fold loosely and then roll gently. Hanging is another alternative. When you want to store a silk quilt, the folds must be filled with rolls of acid-free paper and storage should be in acid-free boxes. Ideal temperature is a constant between 60°F and 70°F (16°C and 20°C) and humidity a constant between 55 and 60 percent. In China, silk is stored in cedar wood trunks because wood worms and other insects abhor cedar.

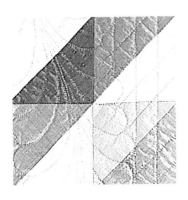

CHAPTER 7

QUILTMAKING WITH SILK

"This quilt was the result of a silk-hunting spree that stretched over a long period. The challenge was to find blues and greens in as many shades and tints as possible. The iridescent weaves of Thai and India silks offer a huge variety, and it was sheer joy to work them into a quilt. The light fabrics offer a variety of textures in whites and off-whites."

Mormor & Morfar's Quilt
Hanne Vibeke de Koning-Stapel, 1992. 82½″ × 51″ (210cm × 130cm). Hand pieced, hand quilted; Indian and Thai silks. Photograph by Sharon Risedorph.

In *Silk Quilts*, I have tried to lift the veil of mystery that makes many quilters reluctant to work with silk. Now that you know more about the virtues of this attractive material, I hope you feel confident to start a small project, putting tiny pieces of silk into one of your patchwork blocks.

FINDING APPROPRIATE SILKS

Experience taught me that it takes time to find silk fabrics that you like, and that you have to spend energy and money to build a collection. Think about all the years it took many of us to form a reasonable collection of cotton fabrics, of which we are not able to use even half, unless we stop buying and make six king-size quilts every year!

I started quiltmaking in 1973, when I lived for a time in the United States. There were not many quilt stores then, and none in my neighborhood. I went to numerous fabric stores and found one or, at most, two cotton calicoes that pleased me in each. Collecting fabric took time and energy. The same is true today of finding silks for quiltmaking. You will have to make an odyssey, searching for what you think you want and maybe finding something else that you cannot resist. When I cannot resist, I buy a small piece, a half-yard (0.5m) or maybe, if totally irresistible, a yard (1m). If I come upon a good background material, I will go for three yards (3m).

I am a traditional quiltmaker, a lover and consumer of big bed quilts. I always start a new quilt with a pattern that intrigues me and with (silk) fabrics that fascinate me at that moment. I am unable to spend weeks planning and designing. I just start and en route I have to solve the problems I encounter by such undisciplined behavior. I never buy more than three yards (3m), and therefore I regularly run out of silk fabric. Afterward, I often realize that running out of fabric and having to create a solution is what adds visual value to my quilts.

The Story of *Stella Antigua*

I want to tell the story of one of my quilts, *Stella Antigua* (see pages x–xi and previous page). When I was browsing for something else, a Liberty silk with peacock feathers stood up and more than attracted my attention. It was prohibitively expensive, but I could not resist and bought about a yard (1m). In my small collection of silks at home, I happened to have at least five pieces of silk in various textures: doupions, crepes, satins, habutais, and Thai silks that matched or nearly matched the colors of the peacock feathers, plus about three yards (3m) of gold Indian doupion that was perfect for the background. I bought three or four additional half-yard (0.5m) pieces of silk and now my color scheme went from golden green to yellow to beige to pink to rose to burgundy—the colors of the Liberty silk.

I cut 2″ (5cm) diamonds in all the colors and flew to the Caribbean island of Antigua, where my eighteen-year-old son had just landed a small, thirty-three-foot sailing boat in which he had crossed the Atlantic. While staying in Antigua, I started to piece the diamonds into one big eight-pointed star. Instead of filling the corners between the star points with four squares and four triangles, I also filled those spaces with 2″ (5cm) diamonds. The result was an octagon which fit perfectly on a small round table at home, on which I placed framed photographs of my dear ones.

My husband did not like this arrangement, and I put the octagon in the cupboard, while thinking of a way to enlarge it into a bed quilt. When I recalled that in many antique eight-pointed star quilts the squares and triangles are filled with appliqué, I decided to enlarge the octagon with eight panels, each 6″ (15cm) wide, filled with appliqué leaves and flowers made from all the small silk scraps. To make the quilt square, I added four two-diamond stars in the corners, all different because I didn't have enough fabric for four similar stars.

Now it was square, but not big enough for a bed quilt. I added four borders, 14″ (34.5cm) wide, each containing four two-diamond stars, plus four three-diamond stars in the corners. Because there was not enough left of the three yards of gold background fabric, I had to look for more. With silks you are never sure to get more of the same, so I had to look for something close. I found a Thai silk that was similar in color but with a smoother texture, which gives a lighter reflection of color.

Looking at that quilt today, I think that the constant shortage of silk fabrics and consequent makeshift contrivances turned into an advantage. Using close options in color and texture adds the vivacity and excitement that meticulous planning might not have achieved.

PROJECT 1
COMBINING SILKS
WITH COTTONS

BLOCK SIZE

15″ × 15″ (36cm × 36cm).

FABRIC REQUIREMENTS

Based on selvage-to-selvage width of 36″ (90cm).

¼ yard (25cm) each of cottons
and silks in six colors, dark,
light, and medium.

For a cautious start using silk in quiltmaking, you might try this
project. I have named this block *Silk Beauty*. My samples are all
machine pieced.

Cut the required number of fabric pieces, using the rotary cutting
diagram, in which a ¼″ (0.5cm) seam allowance is included. To
assemble the block, sew the pieces together in the following
sequence, using the diagram as a guide.

UNIT I

Make one

  1. Sew four triangles B1 to square A to complete one Unit I.

Unit I

UNIT II

Make four

  2. Sew triangle C1 to C2, sew another C1 to C3.

  3. Sew the two triangle units as shown to complete one
     Unit II.

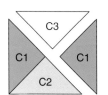

Unit II

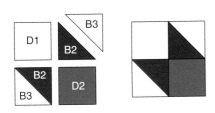

Unit III

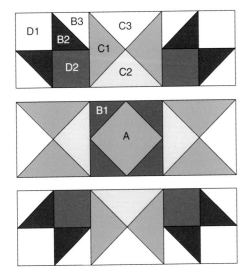

Block Assembly

TIP: If you plan to wash this combination cotton-silk quilt, I recommend prewashing the silk fabrics (before applying the stabilizer), as well as the cottons. Wash the silk fabric in the same way you'll wash your quilt, together with a piece of white muslin. If the silk bleeds and keeps bleeding, it is not advisable to use it.

UNIT III

Make four

4. Sew triangle B2 to B3, repeat.
5. Sew a square D to each no. 4 as shown.
6. Sew together according to diagram to complete one Unit III.

ASSEMBLY

7. Assemble the units as shown.

Make a 15″ (36cm) *Silk Beauty* block following the pattern. Use only cotton fabrics. I used a green chintz, a blue-green and a green plaid, a green and blue print, and two different neutrals. I was pleased with the result.

Next, make a similar 15″ (36cm) block, but replace the dark cotton used in template B2 and the neutral cottons used in templates B3, C3, and D2 with silks. Here, I exchanged the green and blue cotton prints for sparkling green and blue silks, and the neutrals became two different silk neutrals. I liked this block better than the first, and wanted to experiment further.

Make a third block similar to the second block. This time, replace both cottons in templates C2 and D1 with silks. I exchanged both plaids, the blue-green for a sparkling iridescent silk, which enhances the middle part, and the green plaid for a green ikat. The block has become even more vibrant now.

The logical last step in this experiment is to make a fourth block using only silks. It has become a different block with a glowing appearance.

My conclusion is that a patchwork block benefits from even a small piece of sparkling silk, but the character of the block changes completely when only silks are used. I hope you feel confident in trying different experiments now.

Rotary Cutting Diagrams

Square A: cut 1.

Triangle B1: cut 4.
Triangle B2: cut 8.
Triangle B3: cut 8.

Triangle C1: cut 8.
Triangle C2: cut 4.
Triangle C3: cut 4.

Square D1: cut 4.
Square D2: cut 4.

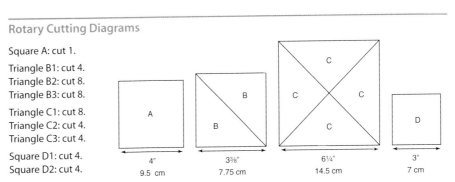

PROJECT 2
ENHANCING COTTONS
WITH SILKS

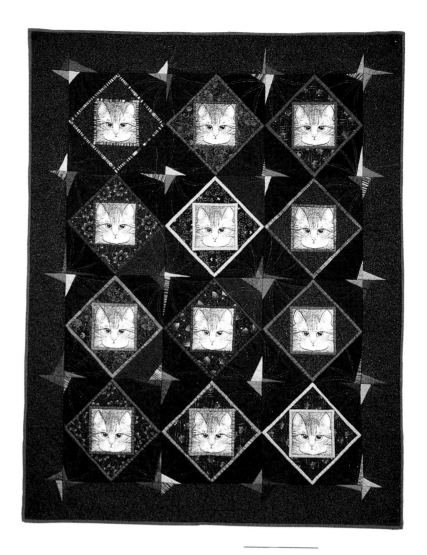

BLOCK SIZE

    $8\frac{7}{8}'' \times 8\frac{7}{8}''$ (21.75cm $\times$ 21.75cm).

QUILT SIZE

    $35\frac{5}{8}'' \times 44\frac{1}{2}''$ (85cm $\times$ 106.5cm).

FABRIC REQUIREMENTS

Based on selvage-to-selvage width of 36" (90cm).

    12 squares, each $4\frac{1}{2}'' \times 4\frac{1}{2}''$
        (10cm $\times$ 10cm), cut from
        preprinted "cat" fabric.

    45" (115cm) of black cotton and/or
        silk fabric in various patterns or
        textures.

    9" $\times$ 9" (25cm $\times$ 25cm) silk fabric
        in 12 colors.

    9" (25cm) silk for binding.

    Thread, backing, and batting.

Cats in the Stars
Machine pieced by Hanne Vibeke
de Koning-Stapel and machine
quilted by Myra-Jane Ibbetson.

In this project I have again used small pieces of silk to enhance the pattern of a cotton print. The *Cats in the Stars* wall quilt features a cat's head, framed with narrow ¼" (0.5cm) strips of lustrous silks in many colors. There are 12 blocks with twinkling star blocks in between. The stars are all silks, the blocks use both cotton and silk fabrics.

Cut the required number of fabric pieces using the rotary cutting diagrams, in which a ¼" (0.5cm) seam allowance is included. Cut 45" $\times$ ¾" (120cm $\times$ 2cm) strips of 12 different colors of silk fabrics. I recommend cutting these strips a little broader than necessary for comfortable sewing, then trim to ¼" (0.5cm) plus ¼" (0.5cm) seam allowance afterward. To assemble the blocks, sew the pieces together in the following sequence, using the diagrams as a guide.

TIP: If you are the lucky recipient of a silk sample booklet or you have a collection of many silk scraps, you are all set to go. Otherwise, look for shop or mail-order remnants, and look into friends' scrap bags. The effect of the shimmering silks is stunning.

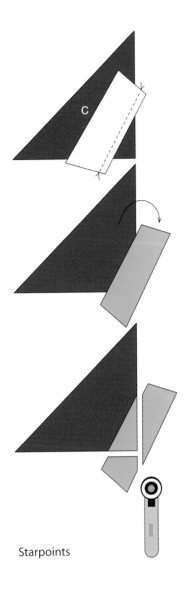

Starpoints

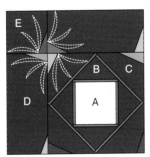

Quilting Diagram

BLOCKS

1. Sew silk strips along each side of square A, butting the corners. Trim back to ½″ (1cm).
2. Sew a triangle B to each side of square no. 1, creating a larger square.
3. Sew four silk strips along each side of no. 2, butting the corners. Trim back to ½″ (1cm).
4. Repeat steps 1, 2, and 3 eleven times to make 12 blocks.
5. Sew a scrap of silk to all triangles C for starpoints. Trim as shown.
6. Sew four starpoint triangles C to each square completed in no. 3.
7. Assemble four rows of three squares each; sew the rows together.

PIECED BORDERS

8. Sew two silk scraps to each rectangle D and one scrap to each square E.
9. Sew two short borders (three rectangles D sewn together) and two long borders (four rectangles D, sewn together with one square E at each end).
10. Sew the two short borders to the top and bottom, and then the two long borders to the sides.

This top is ready to be sandwiched and machine quilted with variegated rayon thread.

Rotary Cutting Diagrams

Square A: cut 12.

Triangle B: cut 48.

Triangle C: cut 48.

Rectangle D: cut 14.

Square E: cut 4.

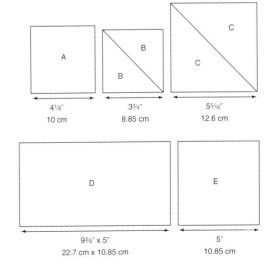

A — 4⅛″ / 10 cm

B — 3¾″ / 8.85 cm

C — 5⁵⁄₁₆″ / 12.6 cm

D — 9⅜″ x 5″ / 22.7 cm x 10.85 cm

E — 5″ / 10.85 cm

PROJECT 3
EXPERIMENTING WITH
SILK TEXTURES

BLOCK SIZE

8″ × 8″ (20cm × 20cm).

QUILT SIZE

27″ × 27″ (66cm × 66cm).

FABRIC REQUIREMENTS

Based on selvage-to-selvage width of 36″ (90cm).

35″ (85cm) medium red silk, fabric A.

25″ × 5″ (65cm × 12.5cm) magenta for inner border.

6″ (15cm) yellow silk, fabric A1.

8″ (20cm) various dark red/ magenta silks, fabric B.

8″ (20cm) various yellows, fabric C.

6″ (15cm) neutral, fabric D.

Thread, backing, and batting.

Silky Queen of Stars
Hanne Vibeke de Koning-Stapel,
1998. 27″ × 27″ (66cm × 66cm).
Machine pieced, hand quilted.

This project, *Silky Queen of Stars*, requires 100 percent silk fabrics and is an experiment in using silk's varied structures and textures randomly. When you have built up a silk fabric collection, you will discover that it is fun to play with the rich, deep colors of silk and benefit from the great variety in the surface textures. I used tints and shades of reds and yellows of Indian doupion, noil or bourette silk, Thai silk, habutai, Indian ikat, and a printed silk, all plain weaves and all commercially dyed.

Cut the inner border: four strips of 23″ × 1¼″ (55cm × 2.5cm). Cut the outer border, fabric A: four strips of 27″ × 3″ (60cm × 7cm). Cut the required number of fabric pieces using the rotary cutting diagrams, which include a ¼″ (0.5cm) seam allowance. To assemble the blocks, sew the pieces together in the following sequence, using the diagrams as a guide.

TIP: For this quilt I chose a silk bourette/noil backing, which I will not do again when I plan to hand quilt. The quilting was not heavy, but because of the thickness of each individual thread in the weave of noil silk, quilting stitches tend to become longer than necessary, especially when working with another noil silk piece on the quilt top. One layer is manageable when hand quilting, but I do not recommend two layers.

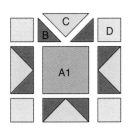
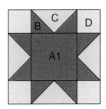

Block I

Block II

Quilt Assembly

BLOCK I
Make four

1. Sew two triangles B to one triangle C; repeat three times.
2. Sew two squares D to no. 1; repeat.
3. Sew two no. 1 to square A1.
4. Sew two no. 2 to no. 3.

BLOCK II
Make four

5. Sew two triangles B to one triangle C; repeat.
6. Sew two no. 5 to one A2.
7. Sew two Block I to Block II; repeat.
8. Sew two Block II to either side of Square A1 in the order shown in the assembly diagram.

Add the border with the mitered corners. Using the quilting pattern on page 169, mark the top, layer it, and quilt it.

Rotary Cutting Diagrams

Square A1: cut 5.
Square A2: cut 4.
Triangle B: cut 48.
Triangle C: cut 24.
Square D: cut 16.

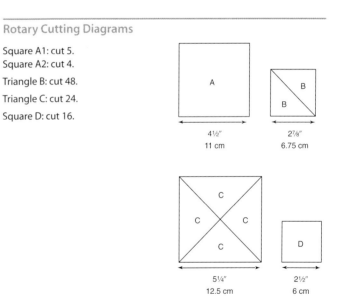

PROJECT 4
EXPERIMENTING WITH THE TEXTURE OF DOUPION SILKS

It is fun to exploit the unique texture of doupion silks, fabrics that are handwoven primarily in India and Thailand. These doupions are reeled from twin cocoons and the principal property–the nubs, slubs, and lumps in the weft yarns–is characteristic. I have found a number of ways to exploit, subtly, this interesting property in traditional quilts, when I have the opportunity to play with triangles. If you have an eye for detail, try these options.

OPTIONS 1 AND 2

Two squares are cut out of a doupion silk, then each is cut into two triangles diagonally, according to the first diagram. These triangles can be sewn to a square and the result is that your eyes move in a circle around the center block. Cut diagonally, as in the second diagram, and added to a center square, your eyes can rest, because the texture of the triangles runs around the center block, either horizontally or vertically. I adapted both options in the triangles of the two- and three-diamond stars in *Stella Antigua* (pages x, 1, and 108).

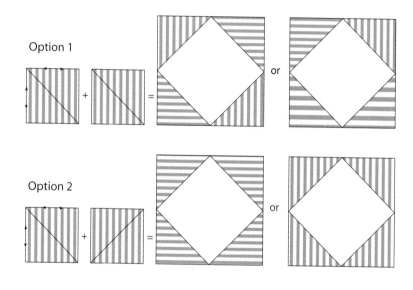

OPTION 3

The same squares are cut diagonally once. Reassembled, they form a large square with an interesting centrifugal effect.

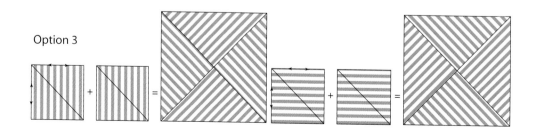

Option 4

Two squares are cut diagonally twice to assemble two quite different blocks. In *Dutch Touch* (page 94) and *Stella Florealis* (page 66), I used these triangles to form symmetrical blocks next to the star blocks, instead of using one whole plain square.

Option 4

If you have made one or several of the small projects in this chapter and discovered the virtues of silk, you may want to venture into creating a whole quilt. Choose your own colors and the amount of silk fabric that will fit your temperament and budget to make one of the patterns in Chapter 8.

SEVEN SILK QUILTS

"When Dutch Touch *was raffled for Amnesty International, I made a smaller version for myself. The size of the feathered star blocks are the same; in* Dutch Touch *there are five rows of each block, which makes twenty-five blocks in a diagonal setting with set-in squares.* Northern Light *has only four blocks in straight setting with a star block in the center. In both quilts all whites are silks, the rest of the fabrics are cotton chintzes and some plaids."*

Northern Light
Hanne Vibeke de Koning-Stapel, 1992. 38" × 38" (97cm × 97cm). Machine pieced, hand quilted. Dutch chintzes and Indian doupion silk. Photograph by Sharon Risedorph.

The seven patterns that follow are arranged in order of complexity, and the first ones are quite simple and easy to sew. All patterns assume some familiarity with quiltmaking; the instructions are not written for the beginner.

The quilts that are constructed in blocks—*Drunkard's Path* and *Stella Florealis*, for example—are easy to make to whatever size you wish by simply changing the number of blocks and arranging them as desired. The number of templates to cut is given for one block.

Drunkard's Path

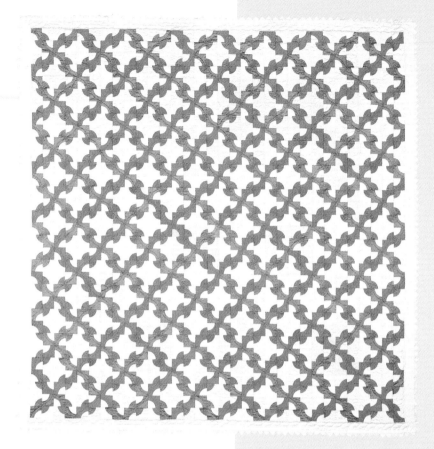

BLOCK SIZE
11″ × 11″ (28cm × 28cm).

BORDER WIDTH
2¾″ (7cm).

QUILT SIZE
93½″ × 93½″
(238cm × 238cm).

FABRIC REQUIREMENTS
Based on selvage-to-selvage width of 36″ (90cm).
10½ yards (9.5m) of white silk.
2¾ yards (2.35m) of white silk for
prairie points.
8 yards (7.25m) of green silk.
Backing, batting, and binding.

This was the second quilt I made, but it was my first silk quilt. I learned that using a fusible behind the silks safeguards the fabrics from fraying.

First cut four borders of 3¼″ × 94″ (8cm × 240cm), then cut the required number of fabric pieces as indicated on the templates on page 161.

BLOCK
Make one

1. Sew one green A to one white B; repeat 7 times.
2. Sew one white A to one green B; repeat 7 times.
3. Assemble the block, following the diagram closely. Make a total of 64 blocks.
4. Sew eight blocks together for each row.
5. Make eight rows, then sew the rows together.
6. Sew the borders to the quilt top, mitering the corners.

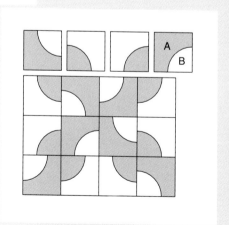

QUILTING

The quilting pattern is French lilies (fleurs-de-lis with French knots) in honor of France and Sophie Campbell, who taught me quilting in Paris. The borders have undulating lines. Using the quilting patterns on page 170, mark the top, layer it with batting and lining, baste, quilt, and bind. I used conventional hand-quilting thread, because silk thread was not available. Instead of binding the quilt, I finished the edges with prairie points, made of 3″ (8cm) squares.

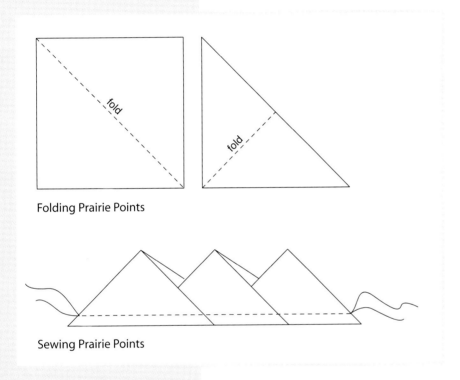

Folding Prairie Points

Sewing Prairie Points

Thai Make Do

BLOCK SIZE

11″ × 11″ (28cm × 28cm).

QUILT SIZE

61¾″ × 72¾″ (157cm × 185cm).

FABRIC REQUIREMENTS

Based on selvage-to-selvage width of 36″ (90cm).

9½ to 10½ yards (8.5m to 9.5m)
of various Thai silks or cottons
in rich color.

Backing, batting, and binding.

The Thai plaids may not be easy to come by, but any other plaid—silk
or cotton—will fit into this easy and quick pattern.

Cut the required number of fabric pieces, using the rotary cutting
diagrams, which include a ¼″ (0.5cm) seam allowance. To assemble
each of the two blocks and the borders, sew the pieces together in the
following sequence.

BLOCK I

Make 15

1. Sew four triangles B to one square A.
2. Sew four triangles C to no. 1 to complete the block.

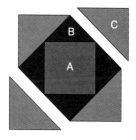

Block I

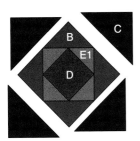

Block II

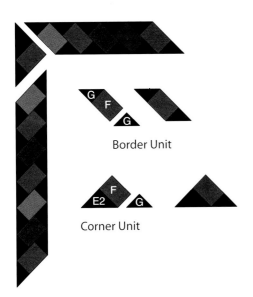

Border Unit

Corner Unit

NOTE: The corners of the photographed quilt are slightly different from those of the diagram. The photographed quilt has one big triangle in each corner instead of one rectangle F, one triangle G, and one triangle E2.

BLOCK II

Make 15

3. Sew four triangles E1 to square D.
4. Sew four triangles B to no. 3.
5. Sew four triangles C to no. 4 to complete the block.

PIECED BORDER

6. Sew two triangles G to one rectangle F to make border unit.
7. Sew 20 border units together for each short border.
8. Sew 24 border units together for each long border.
9. To make a border corner, sew one triangle E2 to one rectangle F.
10. Sew one triangle G to no. 9. Make 4 border corners.
11. Sew border corner to each short and long border.

ASSEMBLY

Sew five blocks together, alternating Block II and Block I, end with Block II. Make three rows. Sew five blocks together, alternating Block I and Block II, end with Block I. Make three rows. Sew the rows together, using the photograph as a guide. First add the two short borders, then the two long ones.

QUILTING

Using the quilting pattern on page 170, mark the top, layer it with batting and backing, baste, quilt, and bind.

Rotary Cutting Diagrams

Block I (to make each of 15 blocks)
Square A: cut 1.
Triangle B: cut 4.
Triangle C: cut 4.
Block II (to make each of 15 blocks)
Triangle B: cut 4.
Triangle C: cut 4.
Square D: cut 1.
Triangle E1: cut 4.
Borders
Triangle E2: cut 4.
Rectangle F: cut 92.
Triangle G: cut 180.

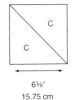

6″
15 cm

4¾″
11.75 cm

6⅜″
15.75 cm

4⅜″
11 cm

3⅝″
8.75 cm

5⅛″
12.5 cm

3¼″
8 cm

2⁷⁄₁₆″
6 cm

4″
9.5 cm

Gijs' Whole Cloth
Crib Quilt

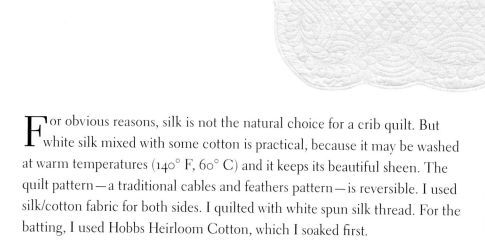

Quilt size
30½″ × 35¾″
(77cm × 90.5cm).

Fabric requirements
Based on selvage-to-selvage width of 36″ (90cm).
36″ × 40″ (90cm × 100cm)
piece of cream-colored silk.
Backing, batting, and binding.

For obvious reasons, silk is not the natural choice for a crib quilt. But white silk mixed with some cotton is practical, because it may be washed at warm temperatures (140° F, 60° C) and it keeps its beautiful sheen. The quilt pattern—a traditional cables and feathers pattern—is reversible. I used silk/cotton fabric for both sides. I quilted with white spun silk thread. For the batting, I used Hobbs Heirloom Cotton, which I soaked first.

Quilting

Wash the fabric and iron it while still damp. Fold the fabric lightly to divide it into four equal parts. The quilting pattern is shown here; the full-size pattern on pages 171 to 175 breaks the design down into four quarter sections. Reproduce this on tracing paper. Mark this portion of the pattern with a hard pencil on the upper left part of the fabric. Flip the pattern over vertically and mark the upper right part. Repeat for the second half-piece of fabric. Layer with batting and backing, baste, and quilt. The space between feathers and cables is quilted in a 90° grid. Cut the edges 1″ (2.5cm) from the quilting pattern, following the round contours of the feathers and cables. Finish with a narrow bias binding.

Northern Light

Block size

17⅞″ × 17⅞″

(45.25cm × 45.25cm).

Quilt size

38″ × 38″ (96cm × 96cm).

Fabric requirements

Based on selvage-to-selvage width of 36″ (90cm).

1½ yards (1.5m) of light silk for the background.

1½ yards (1.5m) of various medium and dark printed cottons and plaids for feathers, starpoints, and narrow borders.

Backing, batting, and binding.

When *Dutch Touch* was raffled for Amnesty International, I made a smaller version for myself. The size of the feathered star blocks are the same; in *Dutch Touch* there are five rows of each block, which makes twenty-five blocks in a diagonal setting with set-in squares. *Northern Light* has only four blocks in straight setting with a star block in the center. In both quilts all whites are silks, the rest of the fabrics are cotton chintzes and some plaids. Making the "feathers" (the two-triangle squares) is time consuming; you may want to use your favorite shortcut method.

Cut the required number of fabric pieces as indicated on the templates on pages 162 and 163, and in the rotary cutting diagrams, which include a ¼″ (0.5cm) seam allowance.

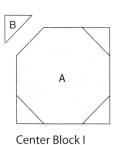

Center Block I

Block I

Make four

1. Sew four triangles B to octagon A.
2. Sew one triangle D1 to one triangle D2; repeat to make 40 squares.

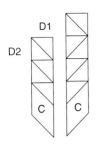
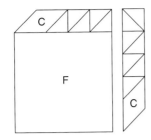

Block I Unit I

Unit I

3. Sew two D1–D2 squares, triangle D1 and diamond C, in order shown.
4. Sew three D1–D2 squares, triangle D1 and diamond C, in order shown.
5. Sew no. 3 to square F, then add no. 4.
6. Make two more identical units. For the fourth unit, add no. 3 and no. 4 to one triangle E.

Unit II

7. Sew two D1–D2 squares together, add one triangle D1, as shown.
8. Sew three D1–D2 units together, add one triangle D1, as shown.
9. Sew one no. 7 to triangle E. Stop sewing at x.
10. Sew no. 8 to no. 9; stop sewing at x.
11. Sew piece G1 to no. 10.
12. Sew one triangle B to piece G2; sew to no. 11 to make Unit II.
13. Make three more identical units.

14. Sew a Unit I to both sides of a Unit II, backtacking at points y. Overlapping the stitches in points x, sew to the edge; repeat.
15. Sew a Unit II to both sides of the center unit.
16. Sew the three rows together, as shown.

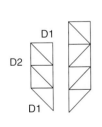
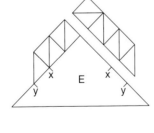

Block I Unit II

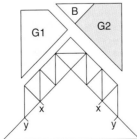

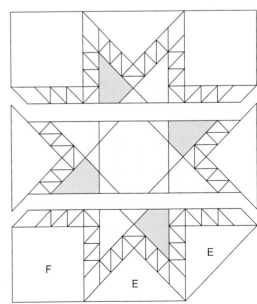

Complete
Block I

Block II

Make one

17. Sew one square H to one piece I.
18. Sew another piece I to triangle J.
19. Sew no. 17 to no. 18; repeat steps 17 through 19 three times.
20. Sew a triangle K to both sides of one no. 19; repeat.
21. Sew four triangles J to octagon L.
22. Sew one no. 19 to both sides of no. 21.
23. Sew one no. 20 to both sides of no. 22, as shown.

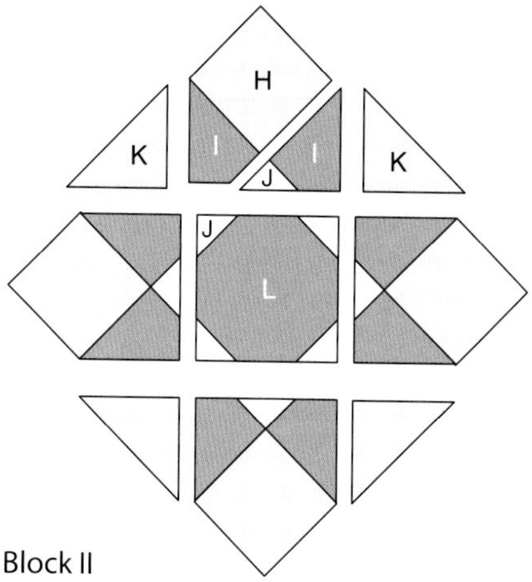
H
K
I
I
K
J
J
L

Block II

Borders

24. Make 124 D3–D4 units.
25. Sew four borders; each has 30 units; sew together as shown.
26. Sew two borders to the top and bottom.
27. Add one D3–D4 unit to each side of the remaining borders; sew borders to the sides of the quilt top.

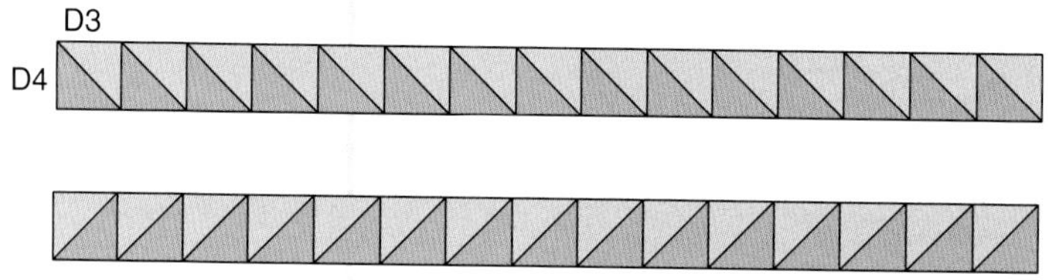
D3
D4

Border

Quilting

Using the quilting patterns on page 176, mark the top, layer with batting and backing, baste, quilt, and bind.

Rotary Cutting Diagrams

Block I (to make each of four blocks)

Triangle B: cut 8.

Triangle D1 (light): cut 56.
Triangle D2 (medium): cut 40.

Triangle E: cut 5.

Square F: cut 3.

Block II (to make one block)

Square H: cut 4.

Triangle J: cut 8.

Triangle K: cut 4.

Borders

Triangle D3 (light): cut 124.

Triangle D4 (medium): cut 124.

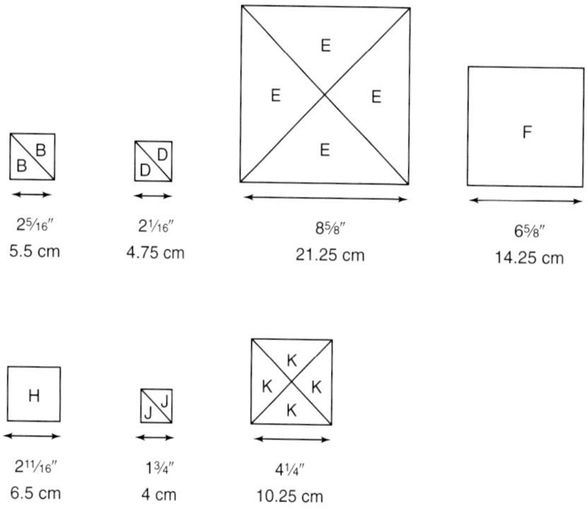
B
B
2 5/16″
5.5 cm
D
D
2 1/16″
4.75 cm
E
E
E
E
8 5/8″
21.25 cm
F
6 5/8″
14.25 cm
H
2 11/16″
6.5 cm
J
J
1 3/4″
4 cm
K
K
K
K
4 1/4″
10.25 cm

Stella Florealis

Block size
17⅛″ × 17⅛″ (43.5cm × 43.5cm).

Quilt size
101⅝″ × 101⅝″
(245.5cm × 245.5cm).

Fabric requirements
*Based on selvage-to-selvage width of 36″ (90cm)
for the silks and 45″ (110cm) for the cottons.*

2¼ yards (1.9m) of chintz fabric.
6½ yards (5.75m) of
   various medium blue and
   green silks.
4 yards (3.5m) of creamy white
   silk for the star background.
4 yards (3.5m) of white silk for
   the border and background.
Backing, batting, and binding.

The polychrome chintz fabric with red flowers, and foliage in many blue and green hues, invited me to use as many medium blue and green silks as I could find, many of them iridescent. The space between the touching stars is filled in with two Indian doupion silks: one chalk-white, the other creamy white. Instead of the usual four triangles and four squares between the starpoints, I chose only triangles, playing subtly with the irregular doupion weft threads. (See also Project 4, page 116.)

First cut the four outer borders (including mitered corners): 5½″ × 103″ (13.5cm × 250cm); then cut the inner borders: 1¼″ × 93″ (2cm × 228cm). Cut the required number of fabric pieces for one star as indicated on the template on page 168, and in the rotary cutting diagrams, which include a ¼″ (0.5cm) seam allowance. To assemble each star block, sew the pieces together in the following sequence, using the diagram as a guide:

1. Sew three rows of three diamonds A together. Make eight starpoints.
2. Sew a triangle B to both sides of each starpoint.
3. Sew two no. 2 together, add triangle C; make 4.
4. Sew two no. 3 together; repeat.
5. Sew two no. 4 together, to complete one star block. Make 25 star blocks.
6. Arrange five rows of five stars each. Sew the rows together.
7. Sew the inner borders to the outer borders. Pin the wide border to the narrow one in the middle, and start stitching from the middle toward the end.
8. Sew the borders to the quilt top; miter the corners.

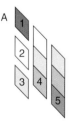

A

Starpoints

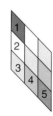

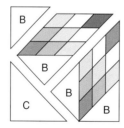

QUILTING

Using the quilting pattern on page 177 and the placement diagram, mark the top, layer it with batting and backing, baste, quilt, and bind it. The border quilting pattern is the same feathers and cables pattern used in Gijs' Whole Cloth Crib Quilt, page 124.

Rotary Cutting Diagrams (to make each of 25 blocks)

Triangle B: cut 16.

Triangle C: cut 4.

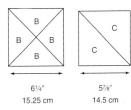

6¼"
15.25 cm

5⅞"
14.5 cm

STELLA ANTIGUA

QUILT SIZE

92″ × 92″ (233cm × 233cm).

FABRIC REQUIREMENTS

Based on selvage-to-selvage width of 36″ (90cm).

10 yards (9m) of silks in at least
seven different light, medium,
and dark hues for diamond A,
M, E, and half-diamond B.

4 yards (3.5m) of silk for the
inner background, panels, and
inner border.

4½ yards (9m) of silk for the
outer background and outer
border.

Backing, batting, and binding.

The story of *Stella Antigua* was told in Chapter 7. The pattern is based on the Lone Star 45° diamond, rendering eight star points in the center. The space between the star points is usually filled in with four squares and four triangles, but in this case it is filled in with diamonds the same size as those used in the star points. This is not a beginner's quilt, because the diamond pattern requires practice in very exact cutting and piecing.

First decide the color placement of the diamonds inside and outside of the starpoints. Then cut the required number of fabric pieces indicated on the templates on pages 164 to 167, and in the rotary cutting diagrams, which include a ¼″ (0.5cm) seam allowance.

NOTE: In order to protect the outer edges while appliquéing, cut trapezoid C with an extra seam allowance of approximately ½″ (1.5cm) on all four sides.

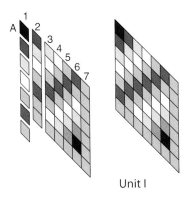

Unit I

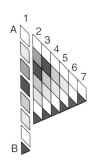
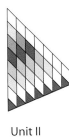

Unit II

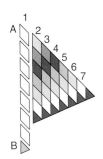
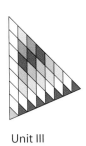

Unit III

Assembling the Units

Unit I

Make eight

1. Sew seven diamonds A together in the order shown to make row one.

2. Follow the diagram carefully and sew each row in the exact order shown. Make 8.

Unit II

Make eight

3. Sew seven diamonds A and one half diamond B together in the order shown to make row one.

4. Follow the diagram carefully and sew each row in the exact order shown. Make 8.

Unit III

5. Sew seven diamonds A and one half diamond B together in the order shown to make row one.

6. Follow the diagram carefully and sew each row in the exact order shown. Make 8.

Assembling the Units

7. Unit I becomes the center of the starpoint; first sew Unit II to the left side of Unit I, then sew Unit III to the right side of the starpoint. Make eight isosceles triangles like the one shown.

Appliqué panels

Make eight

8. Cut eight trapezoids C. (The seam allowance on template C is more generous than usual to allow for adjustment in case of fraying or shrinkage once the appliqué is complete.)

9. Appliqué leaves and vines to all eight panels, using the appliqué patterns on page 179 or patterns of your own design.

Central star octagon

10. Sew one appliquéd C to each isosceles triangle no. 7; repeat seven times.

11. Sew the eight no. 10 triangles together to form the central star octagon.

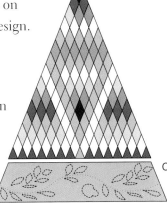

INNER STAR I

Make four

To make one inner corner Star I, you will need two triangles D1, 32 diamonds E, four squares F, and four triangles G.

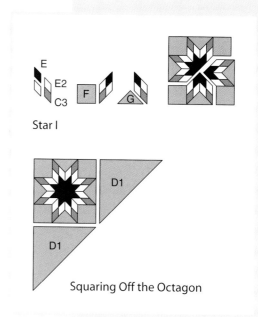

Star I

12. Sew two rows of two diamonds E together to make each starpoint; make eight.
13. Sew four squares F to four of the starpoints.
14. Sew four triangles G to four of the starpoints.
15. Sew no. 13 to no. 14; repeat three times.
16. Sew two no. 15 together.
17. Sew two no. 16 together to complete Star 1.

SQUARING OFF THE OCTAGON

18. Sew a triangle D1 to two sides of each Star 1, as shown.
19. Sew four no. 18 to four sides of the octagon no. 11.

Squaring Off the Octagon

BORDERS

Each of the four borders consists of four Star 1 blocks. For one border Star 1, you will need 32 diamonds E, four squares F, and four triangles G. Repeat steps 12 through 17 to make sixteen Star 1.

For one border, you will need two triangles L; three trapezoids H; one trapezoid HJ1; one trapezoid HJ2; five triangles K; three triangles D2.

20. Sew one H to one K; make five, including one HJ1 and one HJ2, as shown.
21. Sew one HK to one Star 1; repeat twice. Sew KHJ1 and KHJ2 to Star 1 as shown.
22. Sew one triangle D2 to no. 21; repeat two times.
23. Sew four no. 22 units together.
24. Sew one triangle L to either end of 22; make four.

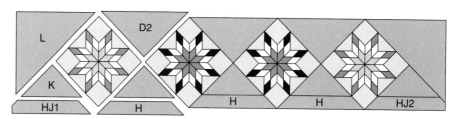

Borders

Star II

TIP: The outside edges of this quilt top are fragile, because of the ¼″ (0.5cm) seam allowance. Either serge the outer border to reinforce before handling, or allow extra fabric on all four sides of the backing, which can be basted over the vulnerable edges of the quilt top—or do both.

OUTER STAR II

Make four

For one outer corner three-diamond star, Star II, you will need 72 diamonds M, four triangles O, three squares N, and one triangle J.

25. Sew three rows of three diamonds M together, as shown. Make eight starpoints.
26. Sew one triangle O to one no. 25; repeat three times.
27. Sew one square N to no. 25; repeat three times.
28. Sew one triangle J to one no. 27.
29. Sew no. 26 and no. 27 together; repeat two times.
30. Sew no. 26 and no. 28 together.
31. Sew no. 29 and no. 30 together to complete Star II, as shown.
32. Sew one Star II to both sides of one border; repeat for the second border.
33. Sew two short borders to the top and bottom.
34. Sew two long borders to the quilt sides.

QUILTING

Using the patterns on pages 178 and 179, mark the quilt top, layer with batting and backing, baste, quilt, and bind.

Rotary Cutting Diagrams

For one Star I
Triangle D1: cut 8.
Square F: cut 4.
Triangle G: cut 4.

For one Star II
Triangle J: cut 1.
Square N: cut 3.
Triangle O: cut 4.

For four Borders
Triangle D2: cut 12.
Triangle K: cut 20.
Triangle L: cut 8.

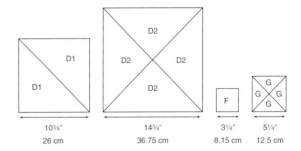

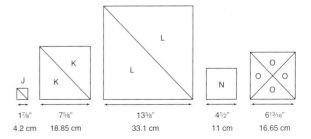

POLYHYMNIA VARIATION— LEMOYNE STAR

BLOCK SIZE

5¾" × 5¾" (14.5cm × 14.5cm).

QUILT SIZE

92½" × 88½"

(235cm × 224cm).

FABRIC REQUIREMENTS

Based on selvage-to-selvage width of 36" (90cm).

10 yards (9.5m) dark silk for the
background.

10 yards (9.5m) of a variety of
medium-colored silks for
the stars and borders.

Backing, batting, and binding.

This pattern is not recommended for beginners because there are no straight lines, and there is a lot of set-in piecing. I first made lots of starry arrow blocks, having fun combining silk plaids and stripes. When 81 blocks with corner squares C (Block I) and 72 blocks without corner squares C (Block II) were ready, I occupied the living room floor for several days, arranging the colorful squares. Pieced together with nine half-Block IIIs, 26 half-Block IVs, and two quarter-Block Vs, the top was ready for the outer borders.

Cut the required number of fabric pieces, indicated in the templates on page 168, adding seam allowances, and in the rotary cutting diagrams, which include a ¼" (0.5cm) seam allowance.

NOTE: Because the top consists of thousands of small pieces, the measurement for the inner borders may vary slightly from mine, which measure ¾" (2cm). Excluding the borders, my quilt top measures 86¹¹/₁₆" × 73" (218.5cm × 201cm). For the outer border to fit, it is essential that, with the inner border added, you end up with a measurement divisible by the length of the long side of triangle G, which is 1⅝" (4.25cm).

Block I

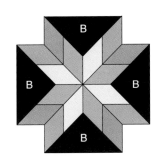

Block II

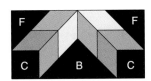

Block III

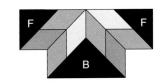

Block IV

BLOCK I

Make 81

For each Block I, you will need eight diamonds A and eight diamonds AR (reversed), four triangles B, and four squares C.

1. Sew two rows of two diamonds A together, as shown.
2. Sew triangle B to no. 1.
3. Sew square C to no. 2; make four.
4. Sew two no. 3 together; repeat.
5. Sew two no. 4 together to complete the block, make 81.

BLOCK II

Make 72

For each Block II, you will need eight diamonds A and eight diamonds AR (reversed), and four triangles B.

6. Sew as Block I without step 3, make 72.

BLOCK III

Make 9

For each Block III, you will need four diamonds A and four diamonds AR (reversed), one triangle B, two triangles F, and two squares C.

7. Sew two rows of two diamonds A together.
8. Sew square C to no. 7; make two.
9. Sew triangle F to the left side of one no. 8 and triangle B to the right side.
10. Sew triangle F to the right side of the second no. 8.
11. Sew no. 9 and no. 10 together; make nine.

BLOCK IV

Make 26

For each Block IV, you will need four diamonds A and four diamonds AR (reversed), one triangle B, and two triangles F.

12. Assemble in the same way as Block III, omitting squares C, make 26.

BLOCK V

Make 2

For each Block V, you will need two diamonds A and two diamonds AR (reversed), and two triangles F.

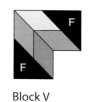

Block V

13. Sew two rows of two diamonds A together.

14. Sew two F to no. 13; make 2.

ASSEMBLING THE ROWS

15. Assemble the rows using the diagram and photograph as a guide, making rows from left to right.

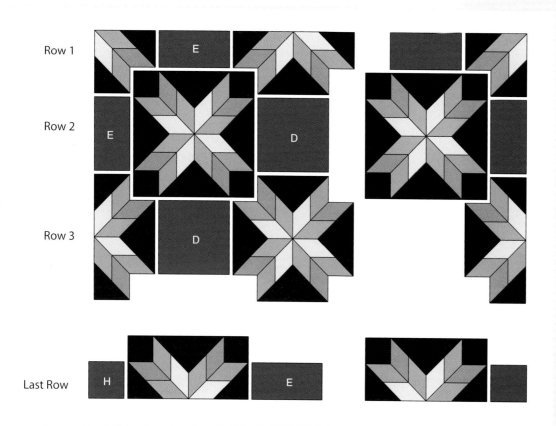

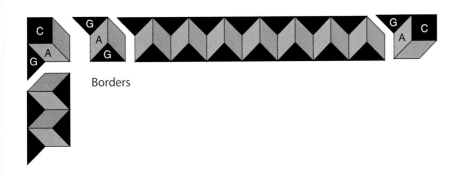

Borders

TIP: The outside edges of this quilt top are fragile, because of the ¼" (0.5cm) seam allowance. Either serge the outer edges before handling, or allow extra fabric on all four sides of the backing, then baste it over the vulnerable edges of the top—or do both.

PIECED BORDERS

16. Sew one diamond A and one diamond AR (reversed) together.
17. Sew one triangle G to no. 18, then attach the other triangle G, making the border unit as shown.
18. Sew the necessary border units together.
19. Sew one diamond A and one diamond AR (reversed), and one square C together to make the corner units. Make four.
20. Sew two corner units to both ends of two of the borders.

INNER BORDER

21. Measure across the pieced quilt top and measure the pieced borders. The difference in measurement divided by two (plus seam allowance) gives the correct measurement for the width of the inner border. Sew the inner borders to the pieced borders.
22. Sew the two short borders to the sides of the quilt top, then attach the two long borders.

Using the patterns on page 180, mark the top, layer with batting and backing, baste, quilt, and bind.

Rotary Cutting Diagrams

For one Block I
Triangle B: cut 4.
Square C: cut 4.

For one Block II
Triangle B: cut 4.

For one Block III
Triangle B: cut 1.
Square C: cut 2.
Triangle F: cut 2.

For one Block IV
Triangle B: cut 1.
Triangle F: cut 2.

For one Block V
Triangle F: cut 2.

Assembly
Square D: cut 153.
Rectangle E: cut 34.
Square H: cut 2.

For one short Border
Square C: cut 1.
Triangle G: cut 101.

For one long Border
Square C: cut 1.
Triangle G: cut 107.

B	C	D	E
B X B	1¾"	3⅞"	2³⁄₁₆"
B	4 cm	9.5 cm	5.25 cm
4⅝"			
11 cm			

F	G	H
2³⁄₁₆"	2⅞"	2³⁄₁₆"
6 cm	6.75 cm	5.25 cm

GLOSSARY

Feathered Christmas Star
Hanne Vibeke de Koning-Stapel, 1995. 36½″ × 36½″ (92.5cm × 92.5cm). Machine pieced, hand quilted; silks and cotton. Photograph by Sharon Risedorph.

Bave The filament thread. See *brin*.

Bourette From French *bourre de soie*, which means floss-silk. It is the waste of Schappe silk, but in sericulture nothing is wasted. Bourette is also called *noil silk*, and it is spun of the very short fibers from the outer and inner parts of the cocoons, including the crushed chrysalides, which are the small brown pits in the fabric. Bourette has little sheen or luster, but it dyes well. In most bourettes/noils, the same yarns are used in warp and weft. Bourette/noil is not as strong as filament silk, but it wears and travels well because it does not wrinkle; it will shrink when washed. Bourette/noil is often called raw silk, although that is a misnomer because raw silk is the filament silk with all the sericin still present.

Bourette Jacquard A noil fabric with a reversible pattern woven into it. Bourette Jacquard silks dye wonderfully. See *Jacquard*.

Bourette satin A heavyweight spun silk with a lustrous and fine satin surface; the back is dull. It contains much of the sheen of *satin duchesse* and is quite expensive, but it is still a waste silk product.

Brin The single silk thread leaving the body of the silk caterpillar through a spinneret. Two brins unite to one *bave*, which is protected by the sericin that hardens on contact with the air.

Broadcloth A plain weave with slight crosswise ribs. Its name comes from the fact that it used to be woven in a broader width than most other fabrics. Now silk broadcloth is mostly a lightweight spun silk, 45″ (110cm) wide, with some luster. Also called *Fuji*.

Brocade An exuberant fabric of the damask family and, like damask, woven on a Jacquard loom. It is richly figured with flowers and foliage; often, silver and gold threads are part of the weave. While damask is reversible and mostly one color, brocade is not reversible and usually contains yarns of more than one color. Brocade is expensive and quite stiff. Small pieces were used in many Victorian crazy quilts.

Broché Embellishment of a weave with additional warp yarns.

Charmeuse See *satin*.

Chiffon From French *chiffon*, which means a rag. Chiffon is a sheer, transparent, soft fabric, made of tightly twisted single yarns in a plain weave. In appliqué quilts, you can fashion three-dimensional flowers and ruches from chiffon. You may also love this material, as I do, for hand-dyed or hand-painted scarves. It's sheer woven wind.

Chirimen An exclusive and expensive Japanese kimono silk. It is a heavy, pebbled crepe silk, in plain colors or woven patterns.

Chrysalis (pl. *chrysalides*). Also *pupa*. A hard brown shell inside which the moth develops. The inactive stage of a caterpillar; when inside the cocoon, it changes into a moth.

Cloqué From French, meaning a crinkled or blistered surface that is obtained by using smooth filament yarns together with tightly twisted crepe yarns. The term *cloqué* is also sometimes used for embossed fabrics. See *embossing*.

Cocoon During metamorphosis, when the change takes place from larva or caterpillar into moth, the caterpillar spins itself into a protective envelope of silk thread. This envelope is called a cocoon. Cocoons are built not only by silk caterpillars, but are a common phenomenon among insects.

Crepe de chine A fabric woven from raw silk yarns that have been highly twisted. When the crepe yarns are used to make crepe de chine, both Z- and S-twists are applied. This makes a strong fabric and gives it a finely structured, crinkly texture with a dulled sheen. Due to a polyester allergy, my husband has for years been wearing silk shirts of crepe de chine. After one day of wearing, I wash them in the washing machine on a wool setting at 85°F (30°C) and they last for years. The word *crepe* derives from a Latin word that means crisp; there are many kinds of crisp crepes.

Crepe satin Art Deco A fabric with a reversible pattern, in this case an Art Deco motif, and a shiny satin finish on the right side. The crepe or dull side is the wrong side. This is the official description, but personally I don't think there is anything "wrong" with the wrong side. This fabric offers a dual advantage to the quiltmaker because the fabric may be used on either side with excellent results.

Crepe satin cloqué A crepe satin fabric, with a relief of blisters, mostly produced by crinkly crepe yarns. The relief may be embossed onto the fabric in a process that uses engraved and heated metal rollers. The "cloqué" effect will not disappear when ironed. See *matelassé*.

Crepe yarns Yarns that are tightly twisted, doubled, and twisted again in both S- and Z-twists. Used as warp and weft in crinkly crepy fabrics.

Damask From Damascus, an important city in Syria on the western end of the Silk Route, but damask was not exclusively woven in Damascus. In China, before the Christian era, damask weaving was done on drawlooms with an intricate system of warp threads that were pulled up in certain patterns by young children (drawboys) sitting on top of the loom. Damask is a one-color reversible fabric with a positive side consisting of floating warp threads in a satin weave, and a negative side that often has a crepe look. As with most reversible-pattern woven fabrics, I find both sides equally attractive. The drawboys lost their jobs when Monsieur Jacquard invented the loom with punched cards that carries his name. See *Jacquard*.

Degumming The process of boiling off the sericin, which is the gummy substance that constitutes about 20 percent of the silk filament, in a hot water bath. See *sericin*.

Denier A unit of weight used to measure the fineness of silk. One denier is equal to a thread or yarn weighing one gram for each 9,000 meters. It may be easiest to remember like this: in a 15-denier silk stocking, only 15 grams of silk are used, so it's thinner and finer than a 40-denier silk stocking in which 40 grams of silk are used.

Dtex The weight in grams of 10,000 meters of silk thread or yarn. See *Tex*.

Embossing An applied process in which silk fabric is pressed between heated and engraved rollers, creating patterns in relief.

Faconné Embellished with small ornaments.

Filament A single continuous silk thread or bave reeled off the cocoon.

Filature The place where the silk filaments are reeled off the cocoons.

Floss The short fibers of the outer and inner parts of the cocoon. Floss is mostly used as embroidery thread.

Fuji A tightly woven plain weave silk with little luster. It has nice body, a medium weight, and is easy to work with.

Georgette A sheer fabric similar to chiffon, but georgette is woven from tightly twisted two- or three-ply crepe yarns, which makes it stiffer and less transparent than chiffon.

Habutai, habutae or *habotai* Japanese name for plain weave fabric in different weights; the name means "soft as down." Often used as lining, but also popular with silk dyers. The heavier qualities are useful in quiltmaking. See *paj* and *pongee*.

Hantoug A handwoven Chinese wild silk fabric, also called "wild pongee." The color is creamy, with a faint tint of pink from the sericin (the gum) that cannot be boiled out completely. Hantoug is one of the less expensive silk fabrics and is useful in quiltmaking.

Hunan or *Honan* A fabric consisting of yarns from both wild and cultivated silkworm cocoons. The warp is mostly cultivated silk and the weft is wild silk. Named after China's Hunan province. This fabric is harder to the touch than most mulberry silks. I like to use it in traditional quiltmaking because of the natural creamy color, but it also dyes very well. When fabrics containing both *Bombyx mori* and wild silk yarns are dyed, the *Bombyx mori* yarns absorb more dyestuff, while the wild silk yarns react differently. This may produce an iridescent or shot silk effect.

Ikat A fabric produced by tie-dyeing the yarns of the warp and/or the weft in certain patterns. The effect is that of a bleeding dye. Silk ikats are produced mainly in India and Thailand. In Uzbekistan, the art of dyeing and weaving ikats is highly developed; men's and women's coats are still made of silk ikats.

Indian doupion or *douppioni* A handwoven fabric, a cottage industry product from India. Handwoven fabrics are always recognizable by the slightly irregular selvage. *Doupion* means that two silk caterpillars have cohabitated in the same cocoon. When reeled, the thread has irregular slubs or lumps, part of the attraction of this material. The warp has much thinner yarns than the weft, which means that doupions will fray parallel to the weft yarns. Most Indian doupion silks are iridescent or shot silks. My experience with doupions has only been positive: the *Drunkard's Path* quilt, made in 1981 from green and white Indian doupion silks, is still in perfect condition. It covers one of our beds and has been taken off every night for more than sixteen years. It was exhibited in the Dutch Silk Museum for nine months, and when it came home there were no signs of sagging. I had the quilt dry-cleaned, with excellent results.

Iridescent silk A plain weave, composed of two different yarn colors, one color in the warp and another color in the weft. The intriguing blend of yarns in shot silk catches and reflects the light in both colors. Regardless of which color catches the light, shot silk fabrics always add brillance and mystery to a quilt.

Jacquard A term often used interchangably with damask. A Jacquard loom is used to weave damask, but the damask fabric woven on a Jacquard loom is often also called Jacquard. Brocades are woven on a Jacquard loom. In 1803, in Lyon, France, Joseph-Marie Jacquard invented the punched card system to mechanically obtain the same sort of intricate pattern weaving that was achieved by using a drawloom with human drawboys, thus eliminating child labor. See *damask*.

Lampas An expensive figured silk upholstery fabric, intricately woven with double warps and wefts on a Jacquard loom, often polychrome; it is not useful in quiltmaking.

Lutestring or *lustring* A plain weave silk taffeta with high luster, originating in France and exported by French Huguenots. The terms are not in use anymore, but used to cover many kinds of lustrous silks in the eighteenth and nineteenth centuries. The high luster was caused by special surface treatments. In England the import of lustring was banned in 1692 when the Royal Lustring Company was formed.

Matelassé From French, meaning quilted, padded, or stuffed. When a silk fabric is matelassé, it is usually a medium-weight fabric with a raised or embossed pattern. Also called *cloqué*. A real matelassé fabric is a weave with a double warp, where the two layers look as if they have been quilted together.

Matka Fabric woven in plain weave of regular Tussah yarns.

Mawata Silk that comes directly from pierced cocoons that are presoaked in hot water and then stretched on a frame. Used by weavers and yarn dyers, they are also suitable for stuffing and cording in trapunto quilts.

Moiré A fabric with fine ribs and a water-wavery pattern, either woven or pressed into it by heavy weight and steam. Expensive and one of the more delicate silks, requiring cautious treatment.

Momme Abbreviated to mm. The Japanese way to indicate the weight and fineness of a yarn per square yard. One momme equals 3.75 grams; 8 mm is lighter than 18 mm.

Mordant Chemical agent used to fix dyes.

Muga A wild silk from Assam in India. The muga cocoon yields a soft, fine, and brilliant filament.

Noil Same as *bourrette*. Noil is the shortest staple of waste silk. Noil is of lesser quality than filament silk or schappe silk.

Organza A crisp, very fine, and transparent plain weave fabric, primarily used in the haute couture industry. Like chiffon, organza is too sheer and transparent to use for quilt tops. Some quiltmakers use it to line and stabilize other silks. It's stiffer to the touch than chiffon because organza may be weighted.

Organzine A strong warp yarn. Raw filament singles are twisted in one direction, then doubled with other likewise twisted filaments, and tightly twisted together in the other direction.

Ottoman A silk with heavy round crosswise ribs. The Turkish sultans who reigned for centuries in the Middle East used to take their midday rest on an upholstered couch, called an ottoman.

Paj Chinese lightweight habutai of 5 to 8 momme or 20 to 24 grams. See *pongee*.

Ply To twist together. One ply is a yarn of several filaments twisted together. A two-ply yarn consists of two of these groups. The gossamer fabrics, such as georgette and chiffon, are made of one- or two-ply yarns. Most silk fabrics are two-ply or three-ply.

Pongee Chinese plain weave silk. In England and the United States, it is called habutai or habutae, which is also its Japanese name. In China the thinnest qualities are called *paj*. It is composed of yarns of both wild and cultivated cocoons. The word means "handwoven" in Chinese. Pongee is not expensive, so it is a favorite of those who like to hand paint on silk and it is a good choice for beginners to experiment with dyeing.

Pongee doupion A wild doupion with incidental slubs.

Poplin, pop(e)lin When the Popes temporarily resided in Avignon, France, in the 1300s, a fabric by this name was woven with silk warp and worsted (woolen) weft, which gave a silky ribbed surface. Ireland later produced the best quality. Now the name of a tightly woven, slightly ribbed cotton fabric.

Pure silk Silk fabric without additives, such as metal salts as mordant or weighting chemical. Often printed in the selvage. One-hundred-percent silk fabric.

Raw silk The name of any silk that retains its protecting gum or sericin.

Sandwashed silk Various kinds of silk fabrics that have been treated with chemicals to achieve a super-soft look, feel, and drape. It is hypersensitive to spots, which are difficult to remove. It was popular in the 1980s, but it is difficult to find today. The reason is that the chemical process of sandwashing makes the silk expensive, but this treatment also affects and corrodes the quality, with detrimental consequences. Wash or home dry-clean a small piece, before spending time and money using sandwashed silk in a quilt.

Sarcenet The name for a silk textile that appears often in old inventories. It was probably first woven by the Saracens in Spain, in either plain or twill weave.

Satin or **charmeuse** A satin weave fabric with a lustrous front and a dull back. It has a glamorous surface of brilliantly shiny silk, due to the long warp floats, and dyes wonderfully in deep colors. Beware of satin's propensity to snagging caused by handling with dry or chapped hands.

Schappe The longer fibers of waste silk, the floss. Also spun silk, degummed by a fermentation process. Sewing thread is often made of schappe silk.

Scroop The rustling sound of taffeta, produced by friction or by chemical additives such as metal salts.

Sericin The gummy substance that protects the single fibers of the silk filament when it leaves the body of the silk caterpillar. Sericin protects the cocoon, keeping its firm vague shape of a peanut.

Shantung A wild silk with slubby crosswise weft yarns. Frequently, it has a cultivated silk warp. Real shantung, named after the province in China, can be recognized by the light blue threads in the selvage and standard width of 33″ (85cm).

Shot silk See *iridescent silk*.

Silk cotton A mixture of 60 percent silk and 40 percent cotton. It has a lustrous sheen, and it was wonderful to work with when I hand quilted an all-white baby quilt for a grandson (page 124). I prewashed the material at 100°F (60°C). It shrank about 6 percent, but came out of the washing machine as beautiful as it went in. The baby's quilt has been washed out several times, by hand and machine, but it still looks new. I also favor the use of this material for my quilt backings, dyeing it the desired color in the washing machine.

Silk hemp A mixture of 40 percent silk and 60 percent hemp, one of many attractive fabrics composed of mixed fibers, in this case combining the luster of silk with the rough texture of hemp.

Slub A soft, thick, uneven section in a yarn or thread.

Spun silk Also called **waste silk**. The short fibers of the inner or outer parts of the cocoons that cannot be reeled, or of pierced and misformed cocoons. These fibers are carded and spun.

S-twist A twist from left to right in yarn or thread. See *Z-twist*.

Tabby Synonymous with plain weave, but also the name of a plain weave fabric heavier than lustring and thicker than taffeta. In England it used to be a silk taffeta with an irregular, watered or waved finish, called moiré, effected by a calendering process. Tabby may also be a corruption of the word Attabi, a textile district in Baghdad where striped and ikat silks were produced.

Taffeta From *taftah* or *taftan*, as the Persians called this fabric, which they wove in ancient times. It is a smooth, tightly woven fabric with slightly thinner warp than weft yarns. Yarn-dyed taffeta has more rustle or scroop than piece-dyed taffeta. However, in the late 1800s the fashionable rustle came from weighting the silk with metal salts, which caused most of the taffetas of that period to perish completely to dust. This kind of silk is also called dynamited silk. Fortunately for silk lovers and quiltmakers of today, the practice of weighting is no longer used. Several authorities, including the International Silk Association in Lyon, France, have assured me that treatment of silks (with the exception of organza) with metal salts has been abandoned.

Tea dyeing Very often applied in traditional cotton quiltmaking, when a fabric needs patina. The protein fibers, wool and silk, absorb dyes and the color agent tannin (in tea) more readily than cellulose fibers such as cotton. The procedure is the same as for cotton; I often add a drop of either yellow or red dye, which gives warm shades.

Tex The weight in grams of 1,000 meters.

Thai silk A handwoven fabric in plain weave, with similarities to India silks. However, Thai silk is much more regular and smooth in texture, and also more expensive. It comes in various weights and is often irides-cent, with different colors in the warp and weft. The Thai silk industry's production before the Second World War was entirely for the home market. Toward the end of the war, the American architect Jim Thompson was assigned to a military mission in Thailand. By the time the war in the Far East had ended, Thompson had fallen in love with Thailand, its artifacts, and its silks. He gave the silk home industry a large boost when he formed the Thai Silk Company Ltd. in Bangkok to make high-quality silks for international export. In 1967 he vanished mysteri-ously on a trip to the Cameron Highlands in Malaysia.

Thread Several strands of fiber with little twist.

Throw From Anglo-Saxon *thrawan*, to twist. In throwing mills the raw, reeled filaments are twisted and doubled in S- and/or Z-twists to make a strong yarn.

Tram Two or more raw filament threads, thrown together in only one direction. Tram is usually used as weft yarns, as opposed to organzine, which is a warp yarn.

Tsumugi An exclusive Japanese kimono silk. Two places are famous for hand weaving beautiful tsumugi: Oshima and Yuki.

Twill A strong fabric in which the crosswise threads pass over and under two or more lengthwise threads. This weave produces ribs in diagonal lines. The right side is the side where the ribs run from below left to upper right.

Tussah Mainly produced in India, a heavy, plain weave fabric with thin warp and thick, irregular weft threads. Tussah silk comes from the large brown cocoons of various wild silkmoths that live in the wild on a menu of leaves of oak, fig, and jujube trees. Their natural colors, derived from the tannin in the leaves, vary in many attractive shades of honey. Most tussahs are difficult to dye. In order to absorb dyes well, most of the sericin must be boiled off, and that is not always possible with this kind of fiber. The remaining sericin makes the fabric hard to the touch. Certain wild silks are bleached and then dyed. In some tussahs, a cultivated silk warp is used. Tussahs fray badly, but cutting parallel to the selvage helps. More than for any other kind of silk, stabilizing with a fusible interfacing is necessary. I especially like to use tussahs in crazy patchwork. Wild silk is often erroneously called raw silk. See *raw silk*.

Warp and **weft** Warp yarns are extended lengthwise on a loom; weft yarns are the crosswise yarns.

Wild silk Silk fibers produced by living-in-the-wild silk spinners of the *Saturniidae* family. The tussah moths, together with the Chinese and Japanese oak silkmoths, are responsible for the biggest production of wild silk. These species live, more or less protected by silk farmers, in jungles and forests; they are semidomesticated. Their cocoons are large and brown; the moths are also much larger and more beautiful than the cultivated silk moth, the *Bombyx mori*. See also *tussah*.

Yarn Several strands of fibers with S-twist and/or Z-twist.

Z-twist A twist from right to left in yarn or thread. Sewing machines are built for threads with Z-twist. See *S-twist*.

BIBLIOGRAPHY

Adebahr-Dörel, L., and U. Völker. *Von der Faser zum Stoff.* Hamburg, Germany: Dr. Felix Büchner, 1994.

Berenson, Kathryn. *Quilts of Provence. The Art and Craft of French Quilt-making.* New York: Henry Holt and Company, 1996.

Bonavia, Judy, and Jacky Yip. *The Silk Road.* London: Harrap Ltd., 1988.

Brügger, Xaver, A. Faes, and P. Willi. *Seiden-Fibel.* Zürich, Zwitserland: Zürcherische Seidenindustrie-Gesellschaft, 1986.

Carboni, Paolo. *Silk Biology, Chemistry and Technology.* London: Chapman, 1952.

Colby, Averil. *Patchwork.* London: B. T. Batsford Ltd., 1958.

———. *Quilting.* London: B. T. Batsford, Ltd., 1972.

Comstock, F. G. *A Practical Treatise on the Culture of Silk, Adapted to the Soil and Climate of the United States.* Hartford: P. B. Gleason and Co., 1839.

Dingjan-Laarakker, Lea. *Ban Reng Khai, A Village in Thailand.* Bangkok: Lea Dingjan-Laarakker, 1992.

Drège, Jean-Pierre. *Marco Polo en de zijderoute.* Paris: Gallimard, 1989.

Feltwell, John. *The Story of Silk.* New York: St. Martin's Press, 1990.

Fitzrandolph, M., and F. M. Fletcher. *Quilting: Traditional Methods and Design.* Leicester, England: Reeves Dryad Press, 1972.

Fox, Sandi. *Wrapped in Glory: Figurative Quilts and Bedcovers 1700–1900.* Los Angeles County Museum of Art. London: Thames and Hudson, Ltd., 1990.

Gaddum, H. T., & Co., Ltd. *Silk: How and Where It Is Produced*. Stockport, England: Chorlton & Knowles Ltd., 1989.

Gwinner, Schnuppe von. *The History of the Patchwork Quilt*. West Chester, Pennsylvania: Schiffer Publishing Ltd., 1988.

Hofenk de Graaff, Judith H. *Geschiedenis van de textieltechniek*. Amsterdam: Centraal Laboratorium voor Onderzoek van Voorwerpen van Kunst en Wetenschap, 1992.

Honda, I. *The Silk Industry of Japan*. Tokyo: The Imperial Tokyo Sericultural Institute, 1909.

Hopkirk, Peter. *Foreign Devils on the Silk Road*. London: Oxford University Press, 1980.

Kolander, Cheryl. *A Silkworker's Notebook*. Loveland, Colorado: Interweave Press, 1985.

Leggett, William F. *The Story of Silk*. New York: Lifetime Editions, 1949.

Little, Frances. *Early American Textiles*. New York: The Century Co., 1931.

MaClagan, Eric. *Notes on Quilting*. London: Victoria and Albert Museum, Department of Textiles, 1932.

Manchester, H. H. *The Story of Silk and Cheney Silks*. South Manchester, Connecticut: Cheney Brothers Silk Manufacturers, 1922.

Montgomery, Florence M. *Textiles in America, 1650–1870*. New York: W. W. Norton & Co., 1984.

Moonen, An. *Quilts: een Nederlandse traditie* (the Dutch tradition). Arnhem, Netherlands: Openluchtmuseum, 1992.

———. *'t is al Beddegoet: Nederlandse Antieke Quilts 1650–1900*. Warnsveld, Netherlands: Uitgeverij Terra, 1996.

Orlofsky, Patsy. *The Collector's Guide for the Care of Quilts in the Home*. San Francisco, California: The Quilt Digest 2, Kiracofe and Kile, 1984.

Orlofsky, Patsy and Myron. *Quilts in America*. New York: Abbeville Press, 1992.

Parker, Julie. *All About Silk: A Fabric Dictionary & Swatchbook*. Seattle, Washington: Rain City Publishing, 1991.

Rae, Janet. *The Quilts of the British Isles*. New York: E. P. Dutton, 1987.

Robson, Scott, and Sharon MacDonald. *Old Nova Scotian Quilts*. Province of Nova Scotia, Canada: Copublished by the Nova Scotian Museum and Nimbus Publishing Ltd., 1995.

Schmidt, Heinrich. *Alte Seidenstoffe*. Braunschweig, Germany: Klinkhardt & Biermann, 1958.

Scott, Philippa. *The Book of Silk*. New York: Thames & Hudson, 1993.

Silbermann, H. *Die Seide: ihre Geschichte, Gewinnung und Verarbeitung*. Dresden, Germany: 1897.

Smit, Jo. *Geillustreerde Internationale Weefdictionaire*. Haarlem, Netherlands: Uitgeverij Fostrum BV, 1981.

Timmerman, I. *Die Seide Chinas: eine Kultuurgeschichte am seidenen Faden.* Cologne, Germany: Eugene Diederichs Verlag, Köln, 1986.

Thornton, P. *Baroque and Rococo Silks.* London: Faber and Faber, 1965.

Wardle, T. *Monograph on the Tusser and other wild silks of India, descriptive of the objects and specimens exhibited in the India section of the Paris Exhibition.* Manchester, England: John Heywood, 1878.

Wayland Barber, E. *Woman's Work: the First 20,000 years. Woman, Cloth and Society in Early Times.* New York: W. W. Norton & Co., 1994.

Whitfield, Roderick, and Anne Farrer. *Caves of the Thousand Buddhas.* London: British Museum Publications Ltd., 1990.

Books on Silk Dyeing and Painting

Buffington, Adriene. *Hand-Dyed Fabric Made Easy.* Bothell, Washington: That Patchwork Place, 1996.

Els-Dubelaar, Ria van. *Zijde: stof tot verven.* de Bilt, Netherlands: Canteclaer BV, 1992.

Hahn, Susanne. *Seidenmalerei als Kunst und Hobby.* Niedernhausen, Germany: Falken-Verlag GmbH, 1987.

Johnston, Ann. *Dye Painting!* Paducah, Kentucky: American Quilter's Society, 1992.

Mori, Joyce, and Cynthia Myerberg. *Dyeing to Quilt.* Lincolnwood, Illinois: The Quilt Digest Press, 1997.

Porcella, Yvonne. *Colors Changing Hue.* Lafayette, California: C&T Publishing, 1994.

——. *Sixcolorworld.* Lafayette, California: C&T Publishing, 1997.

Tuckman, Diane, and Jan Janas. *The Complete Book of Silk Painting.* Cincinnati, Ohio: North Light Books, F&W Publications, 1992.

——. *Creative Silk Painting.* Cincinnati, Ohio: North Light Books, F&W Publications, 1995.

Catalogs, Articles, and Other Publications

Aramco Corp. "Traveling the Silk Roads." *Aramco World,* 1988.

Backman, Maggie. "Misunderstood Silk." *Craft and Needlework,* February 1994.

——. "Why Knot Silk?" *Craft and Needlework,* March 1994.

Beukers, Henriette. "Van alles over zijde." *Handwerken Zonder Grenzen*: 4. Utrecht, Netherlands: Kluwerpers BV, 1984.

Brochure "La Soie" with the cooperation of Mr. R. Currie. Lyon, France: International Silk Association.

Cannella, Deborah. "The Story of Gertrude Rapp: Piety, Prosperity, and Lovely Silk Ribbons." *Piecework*, July/August 1994.

Daurelle, Jude. "The Silk Industry in Utah: Produce What You Consume." *Piecework*, July/August 1994.

Exhibition catalog. "Couleurs des Quatre Saisons. Costumes et Pojagi de Corée à l'époque Chŏson." Morlanwelz, Belgium: Musée Royal de Mariemont, 1996.

Exhibition catalog. "Embroidered Quilts from the Museu Nacional de Arte Antiga [Lisboa.]—India, Portugal, China 16th–18th Century." London: Kensington Palace, 1978.

Exhibition catalog. "Manteau de Nuages. Kesa Japonais, XVIII–XIX e siècles." Paris: Musée National des Arts Asiatique-Guimet, Paris, 1992, and Musée des Tissus, Lyon, France, 1991–1992.

Exhibition catalogue. "Profusion of Color: Korean Costumes Wrapping Cloth of the Chŏson Dynasty. Asian Art Museum of San Francisco and the Korean Museum of Embroidery." Seoul, Korea, 1995.

Flensburg, H., and I. Hammers. "Basel Naturseide und ihre Veredlung." *Textil Praxis International*, July 1988.

Frost Steen, Mary. "To Utilize Every Idle Hand: Silk Culture in the United States." *Spin-Off*, Summer 1994.

——. "A Dress for Two Worlds: The Story of Eliza Lucas Pinckney." *Piecework*, November/December 1996.

Hanyu, Gao. "Technical and Artistic Development of Chinese Patterned Silk." Shanghai Academy of Textile Research, 1994.

Markowsky, Barbara. "Europäische Seidengewebe des 13–18 Jahrhunderts." Kat. Kunstgewerbemuseum der Stadt Köln, 1976.

Seide. *Deutsches Textilforum*. Heft 2:83, June 1983.

Walter, Reinhard. "Dyeing of Wool, Wool Blends and Silk." Frankfurt am Main, Germany: DyStar Textilfarben GmbH & Co. (Business Unit of Bayer & Hoechst), November 1995.

Zahn, H., B. Wulfhorst, and M. Steffens. "Seide (Maulbeerseide)—Tussah-seide." Düsseldorf, Germany: *Chemiefasern/Textilindustrie*, January/February 1994.

RESOURCES

United States

Britex Fabrics

146 Geary Street
San Francisco, California 94108
Phone: (415) 392-2910

Huge collection of silk fabrics and silk ribbons. Various silk threads. Mail order for personalized swatch service

G-Street Fabrics

Sully Station Shopping Center
5077 Westfields Boulevard
Centreville, Virginia 20120
Phone: (703) 818-8090

Vast array of silk fabrics and notions

G-Street Fabrics

Mid-Pike Plaza
11854 Rockville Pike
Rockville, Maryland 20852
Phone: (301) 231-8998

Vast array of silk fabrics and notions

Pieces of Eight/Dianne Smith
>P.O. Box 4306
>South Colby, Washington 98384
>Phone: (360) 871-7756

Wonderful selection of hand-dyed silks

Quilters' Resource Inc.
>P.O. Box 148850
>Chicago, Illinois 60614
>Phone: (800) 676-6543

Silk batting

Thai Silks
>252 State Street
>Los Altos, California 94022
>Phone: (415) 948-8611

Mail-order catalog, samples of huge collection of silk fabrics at great prices

Things Japanese/Maggie Backman
>9805 N.E. 116th Street, Suite 7160
>Kirkland, Washington 98034-4248
>Phone: (206) 821-2287
>Fax: (206) 821-3554

Tire Thread (Japanese filament thread) in many colors. Books on silk painting and dyeing

Europe

Please check with an international operator for correct use of international phone numbers.

Ponsard Frères
>7&9 Boulevard du Temple
>75003 Paris, France
>Phone: Country code 33, 01 42 72 56 40
>Fax: Country code 33, 01 42 72 56 50

Huge choice of dyes and white silks for dyeing.

PSR Quilt
>15, rue de Londres
>89000 Saint Georges
>Sur Baulche, France
>Phone: Country code 33, (03) 86 46 98 04
>Fax: Country code 33, (03) 86 46 50 84

Silk battings

Seiden-Reinhard

Löwengrube am Dom

80333 Munich, Germany

Phone: Country code 49, (89) 22 58 43

Retail silks only

Seiden-Reinhard

Postfach 10 12 64

80333 Munich, Germany

Wholesale goods

Roisin Cross Silk

88 Whitebeam Road

Clonskeagh

Dublin 14, Ireland

Phone: Country code 353, 1 694 080

Capsicum

Oude Hoogstraat 1

1012 CD Amsterdam

Netherlands

Phone: Country code 31, (20) 623 10 16

Direct import of silks and cottons from the Far East

Cotton & Silk

Frederikstraat 481

2514 LN the Hague, Netherlands

Phone: Country code 31, (70) 345 17 19

Many kinds of interior decorator's silks and cottons

Michel Stoffen

Lijnmarkt 42

3511 KJ Utrecht, Netherlands

Phone: Country code 31, (030) 231 80 21

Retail Indian doupion silks, at least two hundred kinds, at very reasonable prices

Shantoeng

P.O. Box 175

8800 AD Franeker, Netherlands

Phone: Country code 31, (517) 395 229

Retail outlet of Zijdar (see description)

Zijdar
> P.O. Box 203
> 8800 AE Franeker, Netherlands
> Phone: Country code 31, (517) 395 229

Wholesaler; specializes in silk paints and dyes, and white silks for painting and dyeing

The G & G Quilt Company
> 52 Swan Lane
> Coventry CV2 4GB, United Kingdom
> Phone and fax: Country code 44, 1203 227 011

Mail-order silk wadding

Silks for Handspinners/Sue Harris
> Tregoyd Mill, Three Cocks
> Brecon, Powys
> Wales LD3 0SW, United Kingdom
> Phone and fax: Country code 44, 1497 847 421

Silk batting and white silk ribbon

The Silk Route/ Hilary Williams
> 32 Wolseley Road
> Godalming
> Surrey GU7 3EA, United Kingdom
> Phone: Country code 44, 1483 420 544

Unusual and textured silk fabrics and threads

Texere Yarns
> College Mill, Barkerend Road
> Bradford BD3 9AQ, United Kingdom
> Phone: Country code 44, 1274 722 191
> Fax: Country code 44, 1274 393 500

Silk yarns and thread

Whaleys (Bradford) Ltd.
> Harris Court, Great Horton
> Bradford
> West Yorkshire BD7 4EQ, United Kingdom
> Phone: Country code 44, 1274 576 718
> Fax: Country code 44, 1274 521 309

Silk mail order and "prepared for dyeing" white silks

In Kyoto, Japan, the best place to buy Japanese kimonos is at open market in Toji, held the twentieth of every month.

INDEX

Page numbers in boldface are for artwork and photographs.

TEMPLATES

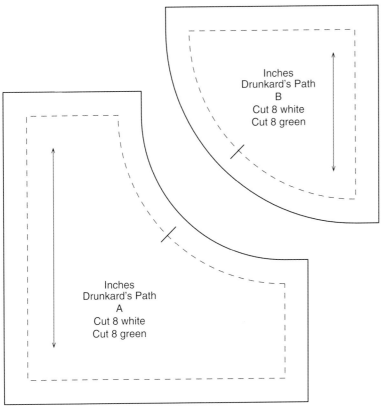

Inches
Drunkard's Path
B
Cut 8 white
Cut 8 green

Inches
Drunkard's Path
A
Cut 8 white
Cut 8 green

DRUNKARD'S PATH

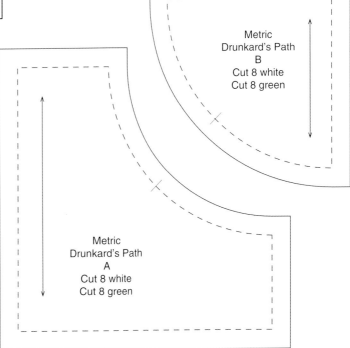

Metric
Drunkard's Path
B
Cut 8 white
Cut 8 green

Metric
Drunkard's Path
A
Cut 8 white
Cut 8 green

Northern Light
(inches)

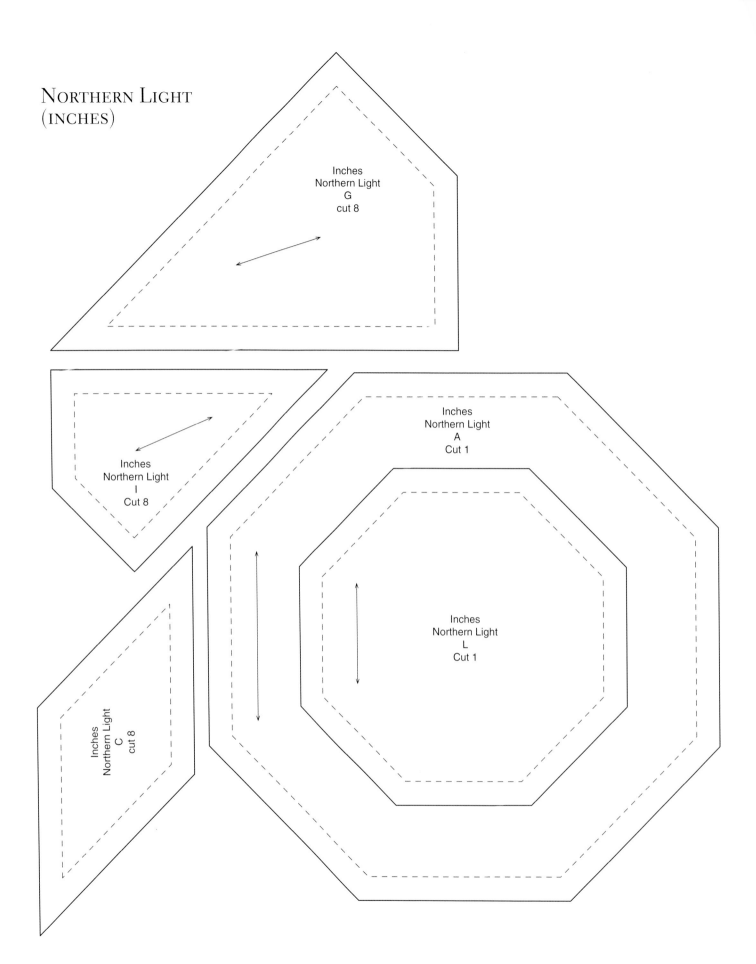

Inches
Northern Light
G
cut 8

Inches
Northern Light
I
Cut 8

Inches
Northern Light
C
cut 8

Inches
Northern Light
A
Cut 1

Inches
Northern Light
L
Cut 1

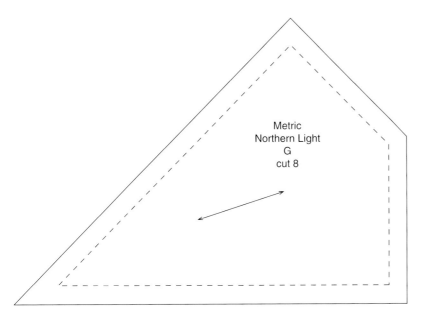

Metric
Northern Light
G
cut 8

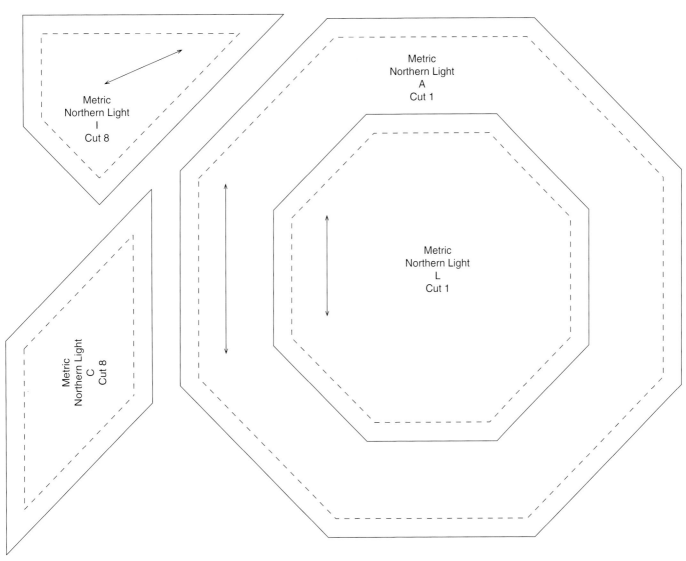

Metric
Northern Light
I
Cut 8

Metric
Northern Light
A
Cut 1

Metric
Northern Light
L
Cut 1

Metric
Northern Light
C
Cut 8

STELLA ANTIGUA
(INCHES)

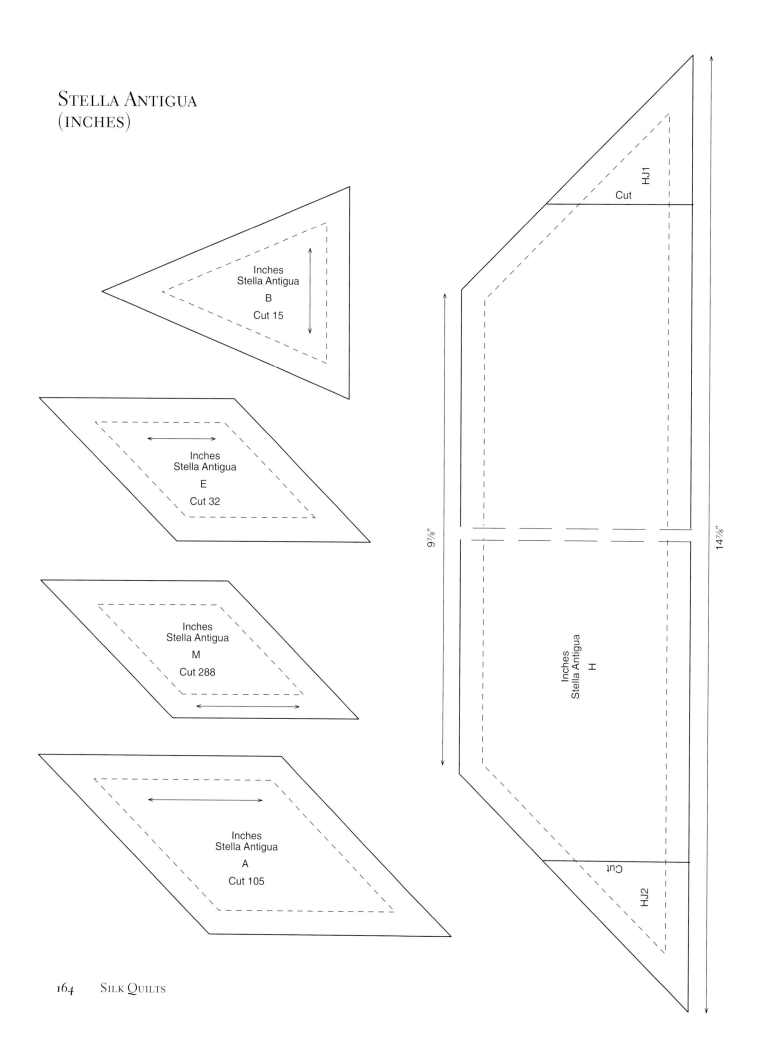

Inches
Stella Antigua
B
Cut 15

Inches
Stella Antigua
E
Cut 32

Inches
Stella Antigua
M
Cut 288

Inches
Stella Antigua
A
Cut 105

Inches
Stella Antigua
H

HJ1

Cut

Cut

HJ2

9⁷/₈"

14⁷/₈"

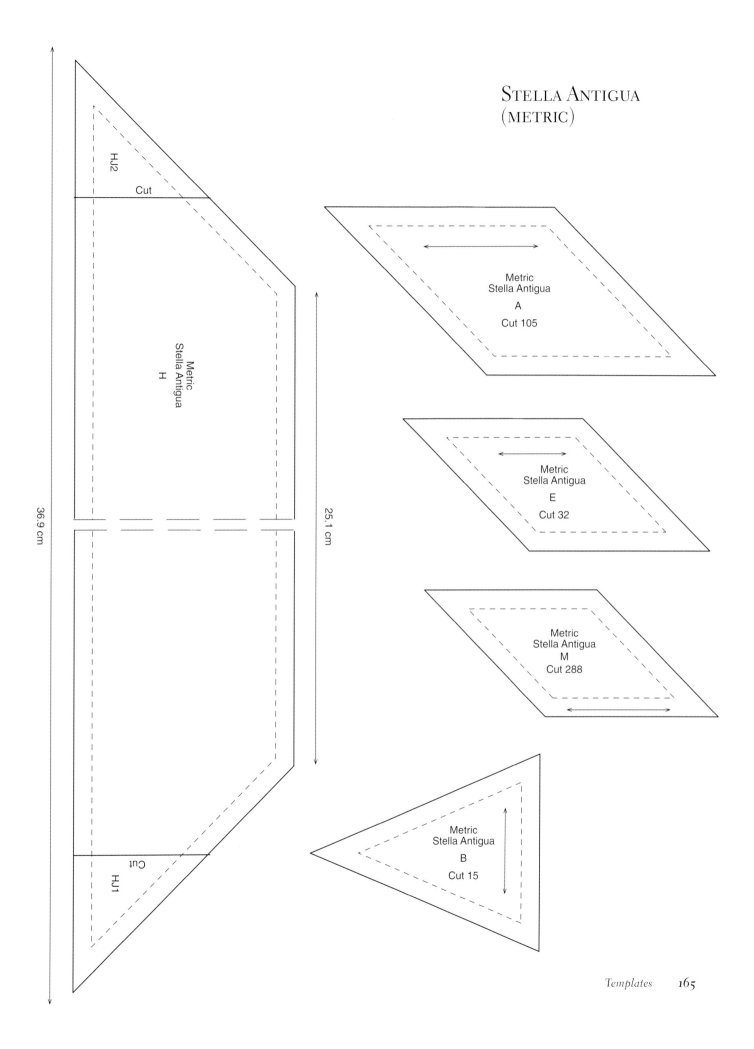

STELLA ANTIGUA
(METRIC)

36.9 cm

HJ2

Cut

Metric
Stella Antigua
H

25.1 cm

Cut

HJ1

Metric
Stella Antigua

A

Cut 105

Metric
Stella Antigua

E

Cut 32

Metric
Stella Antigua
M
Cut 288

Metric
Stella Antigua

B

Cut 15

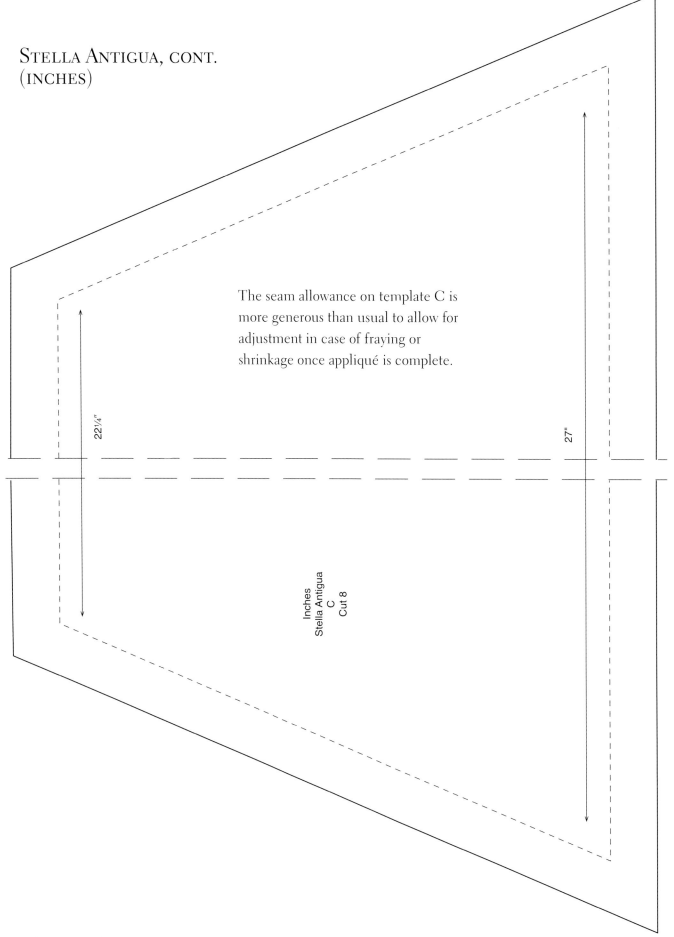

The seam allowance on template C is more generous than usual to allow for adjustment in case of fraying or shrinkage once appliqué is complete.

22¼"

27"

Inches
Stella Antigua
C
Cut 8

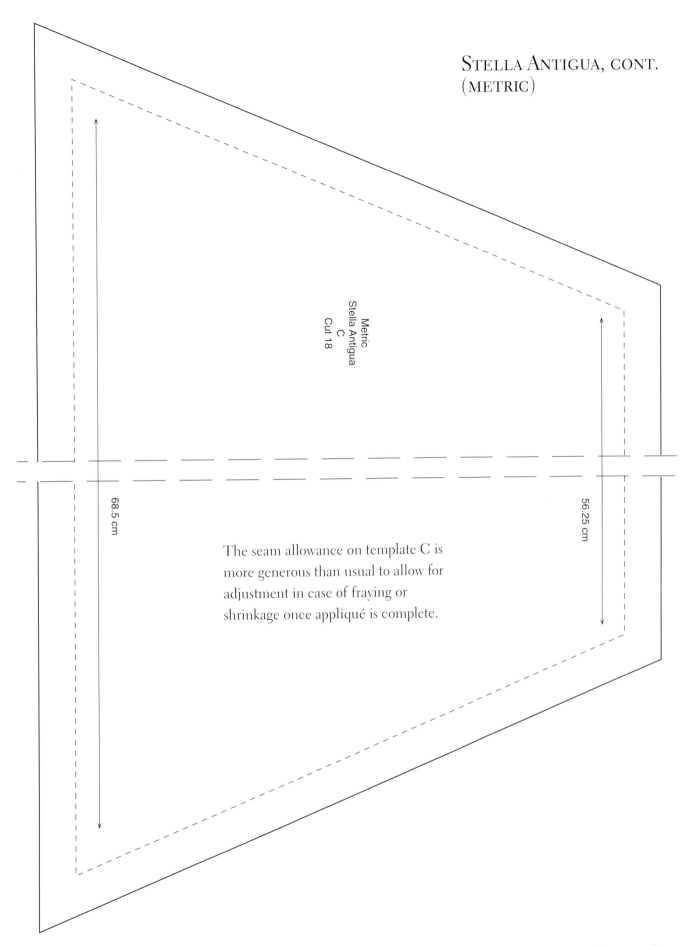

STELLA ANTIGUA, CONT.
(METRIC)

Metric
Stella Antigua
C
Cut 18

68.5 cm

56.25 cm

The seam allowance on template C is
more generous than usual to allow for
adjustment in case of fraying or
shrinkage once appliqué is complete.

Polyhymnia

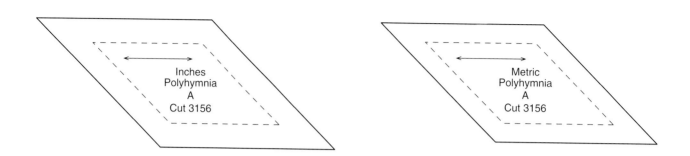

Inches
Polyhymnia
A
Cut 3156

Metric
Polyhymnia
A
Cut 3156

Stella Florealis

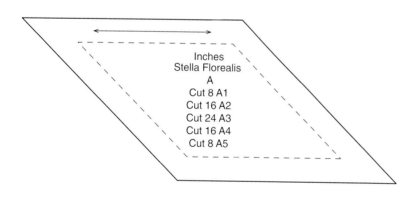

Inches
Stella Florealis
A
Cut 8 A1
Cut 16 A2
Cut 24 A3
Cut 16 A4
Cut 8 A5

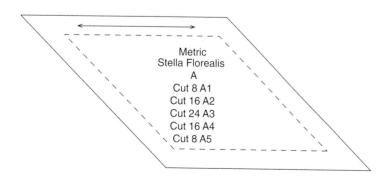

Metric
Stella Florealis
A
Cut 8 A1
Cut 16 A2
Cut 24 A3
Cut 16 A4
Cut 8 A5

QUILTING DESIGNS

SILKY QUEEN OF STARS

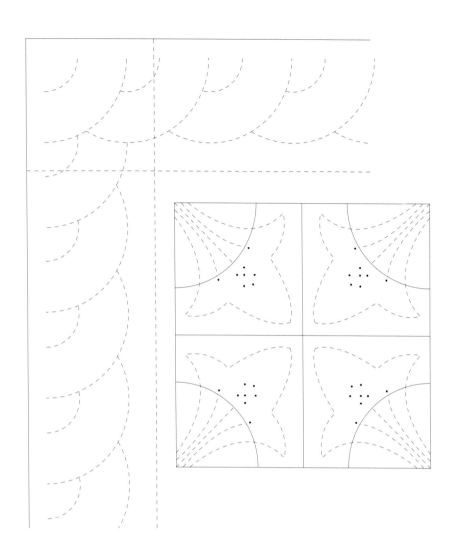

Drunkard's Path

For full size patterns,
enlarge 200%

Thai Make Do

For full size patterns,
enlarge 200%

GIJ'S QUILT, CONT.

One-quarter of actual pattern (Part A)

A	B
C	D

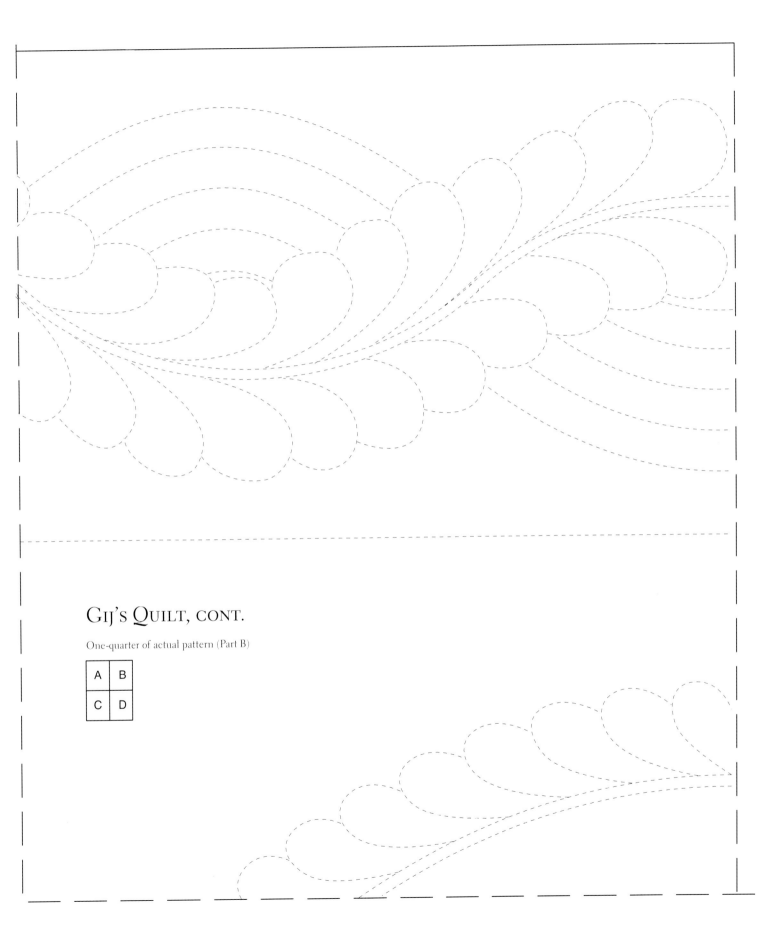

Gij's Quilt, cont.

One-quarter of actual pattern (Part B)

A	B
C	D

GIJ'S QUILT, CONT.

One-quarter of actual pattern (Part C)

A	B
C	D

GIJ's QUILT, CONT.

One-quarter of actual pattern (Part D)

A	B
C	D

NORTHERN LIGHT

STELLA FLOREALIS

For full size patterns,
enlarge 200%

Stella Antigua

Fits in template L

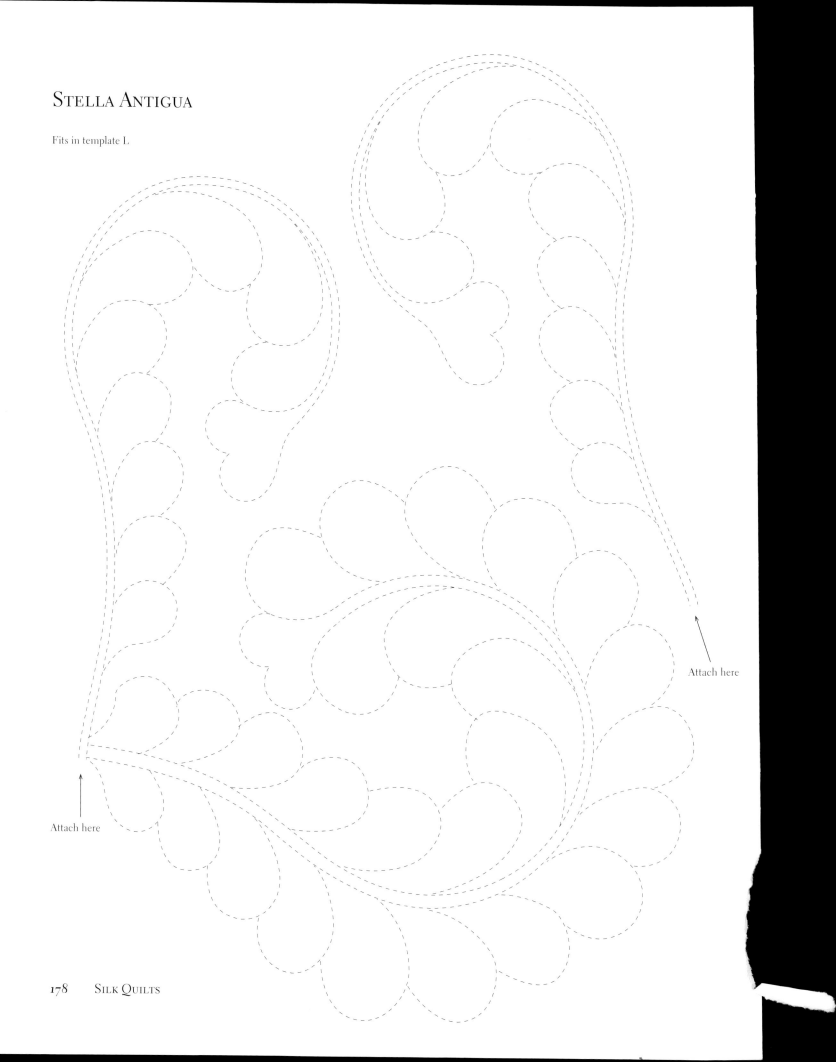

Attach here

Attach here

STELLA ANTIGUA, CONT.

For full size patterns,
enlarge 200%

Stella Antigua
Appliqué shapes

Stella Antigua
Fits in Template D2

Stella Antigua
Fits in Template H